SOUTHWEST INSPIRATION

120 Home Designs in *Santa Fe, Spanish, & Contemporary Styles*

HOME PLANNERS

SOUTHWEST INSPIRATION

Published by Home Planners, LLC
Wholly owned by Hanley-Wood, LLC

President, Jayne Fenton
Chief Financial Officer, Joe Carroll
Vice President, Publishing, Jennifer Pearce
Vice President, Retail Sales, Chuck Tripp
Vice President, General Manager, Marc Wheeler
Executive Editor, Linda Bellamy
National Sales Manager, Book Division, Julie Marshall
Managing Editor, Jason D. Vaughan
Special Projects Editor, Kristin Schneidler
Associate Editors, Nate Ewell, Kathryn R. Sears
Lead Plans Associate, Morenci C. Clark
Plans Associates, Jill M. Hall, Elizabeth Landry, Nick Nieskes
Proofreaders, Douglas Jenness, Sarah Lyons
Technical Specialist, Jay C. Walsh
Lead Data Coordinator, Fran Altemose
Data Coordinators, Misty Boler, Melissa Siewert
Production Director, Sara Lisa
Production Manager, Brenda McClary

Big Designs, Inc.
President, Creative Director, Anthony D'Elia
Vice President, Business Manager, Megan D'Elia
Vice President, Design Director, Chris Bonavita
Editorial Director, John Roach
Assistant Editor, Tricia Starkey
Director of Design and Production, Stephen Reinfurt
Group Art Director, Kevin Limongelli
Photo Editor, Christine DiVuolo
Art Director, Jessica Hagenbuch
Graphic Designer, Mary Ellen Mulshine
Graphic Designer, Lindsey O'Neill-Myers
Graphic Designer, Jacque Young
Assistant Photo Editor, Mark Storch
Project Director, David Barbella
Assistant Production Manager, Rich Fuentes

Photo Credits
Front Cover: Used for many centuries, a kiva fireplace
adds an authentic Southwestern flavor to any home. ©Brad Simmons/Esto
Title Page: ©Getty Images/EyeWire Collection
Back Cover: ©Brad Simmons/Esto

Home Planners Corporate Headquarters
3275 W. Ina Road, Suite 220
Tucson, Arizona 85741

Distribution Center
29333 Lorie Lane
Wixom, Michigan 48393

© 2003

10 9 8 7 6 5 4 3 2 1

Printed in the United States of America

Library of Congress Control Number: 2003105316

ISBN softcover: 1-931131-19-8

New Mexico's Inn at Loretto exemplifies classic multifamily Pueblo dwellings. See page 6 to learn more about the many architectural styles commonly found in the Southwest.

SOUTHWEST INSPIRATION

The red rocks and sand of Monument Valley, located within the Navajo Tribal Park on the Utah/Arizona border, provide an example of the startling beauty of the Southwestern landscape.

LET THE SOUTHWEST INSPIRE YOU

Tall saguaro cacti fill
the Arizona desert.

From the bright lights and busy pace of large cities like Las Vegas, Nevada, to the subtle beauty and cultural centers of cities like Santa Fe, New Mexico, the American Southwest is truly an enticing region. Its year-round sunshine, mild winters, and hot summers—interrupted only by dramatic, powerful storms—combine with its fascinating historical and cultural traditions to create a special allure. Each year, many people visit this region and bring home vivid memories of its magnificence—and, each year, many people are inspired to return and make the Southwest their home. If you're drawn to the Southwest and want to learn more, *Southwest Inspiration* is the book for you.

Learn about this region's rich and varied architectural influences in our "Architecture" section, beginning on page 6; then, turn to page 15 to browse through our photo gallery of stunning Southwestern-style interiors. Another photo showcase, featuring five constructed Southwestern homes, follows. Our plan portfolio—more than 125 professionally drawn plans from eight different designers—begins on page 49 with our "Southwestern Showcase," a selection of spectacular plans presented in full color. Homes in the next two sections, "Santa Fe & Pueblo-Style Homes" and "Spanish Colonial & Mission-Style Homes," are inspired by the architectural traditions of the old Southwest. Completing the collection is "Contemporary Southwestern Homes," made to fit today's Southwestern neighborhoods. With plans from 1,500 to 5,400 square feet, you're sure to find a design that meets your needs. When you're ready to order, turn to page 181 and get started on building your own Southwestern retreat. ■

ARCHITECTURE

The Inn at Loretto, located in
Santa Fe, New Mexico, brings
to mind the classic multifamily
Pueblo dwellings.

SOUTHWESTERN ARCHITECTURE

While using nature as its guide, the diverse architecture of the Southwest mirrors the region's rich history.

Rich with historical and cultural heritage, the best-known home styles of the Southwest draw from a variety of influences: the Pueblo-style designs created by Native Americans, the Colonial, Mission, and Eclectic styles brought by Spanish colonists, and the Territorial designs built by settlers from the Eastern states. Though these popular styles have many elements in common, such as building materials, each style has its own distinctive characteristics as well.

Heavy wooden lintels sit above the windows of this Santa Fe style home; the ladder adds a touch of Pueblo style.

PUEBLO STYLE

Pueblo Style at a Glance

- THICK INTERIOR & EXTERIOR WALLS
- FLAT ROOFS
- EARTH-TONED EXTERIORS
- LARGE CENTRAL HEARTHS WITH BANCOS TO EITHER SIDE
- CEILINGS COMPOSED OF VIGAS AND LATILLAS

One of the most important influences on Southwestern architecture is Pueblo-style housing—in fact, when most people think of Southwestern architecture, they think of the soft lines and solid exteriors of Pueblo homes. The earliest Pueblos, made by Native Americans, were large multifamily homes constructed of adobe—a mixture of earth, straw, and water pressed with frame-

work of rock and timber. Exterior walls were often two to four feet thick, keeping the dwellings cool in summer and warm in winter. The Pueblos also served as a safe refuge for the Native American tribes; windows were small, and there were few ground-level doors. Often, the only way to enter the Pueblo was by climbing a ladder and dropping through a rooftop opening. (This rooftop opening also allowed smoke from the cooking hearth to escape.) Once

the ladders were pulled up, the adobe homes were able to effectively resist attacks.

Classic adobe interiors also displayed unique characteristics. Since adobe is a heavy building material, the Native Americans created extra reinforcement in the ceilings by using vigas and latillas. Vigas—the stronger, heavier timbers—were placed across the shorter portion of the room, and latillas—smaller branch-size

Above: This thoroughly modern Pueblo-style home features plenty of windows. Plan HPT810014; see page 58 for detail.

SANTA FE STYLE

Santa Fe style homes are, in many ways, simply modern adaptations of Pueblo-style homes, with some Spanish Colonial elements as well. During the 19th century, residents of New Mexico wanted their homes to have a unique look, distinct from the Mission-style homes of California. Santa Fe designs incorporate many of the features of classic Pueblo homes. The warm, earth-toned exteriors usually display flat roofs and thick walls; architectural details include heavy, recessed doors, wooden lintels over the windows, and vigas that extend through the walls to the exterior. Courtyards, many with fireplaces, are common as well. Inside, rooms often boast corner fireplaces and gently curved walls with plenty of nichos; ceilings are composed of exposed wooden beams or vigas and latillas, and walls are often a bright, clean white. ■

Santa Fe Style at a Glance

- EARTH-TONED EXTERIORS
- FLAT ROOFS
- THICK INTERIOR & EXTERIOR WALLS
- CEILINGS COMPOSED OF VIGAS AND LATILLAS OR EXPOSED WOODEN BEAMS
- STRIKING WHITE INTERIOR WALLS
- HEAVY, RECESSED DOORS
- WOODEN LINTELS OVER WINDOWS
- FLOOR PLANS WITH GENTLY CURVED ROOMS

This plan exemplifies Santa Fe design with its earth-toned exterior, projecting vigas, and heavy wooden front door. Inside, note the exposed-beam ceiling in the great room and the curved walls of the master suite and breakfast area. Plan HPT810018; see page 62 for details.

pieces of wood—were placed at angles between the vigas. Interior walls were often as thick as the exterior walls, and they were usually covered with a coating of white earth for a bright, clean appearance.

Though some people still build classic mud-brick Pueblo homes today, most modern adaptations of Pueblo homes are built from stone masonry or cement stucco. These Pueblo-style homes retain many of the features of the originals: thick exterior and interior walls, often a bright white; ceilings that showcase vigas and latillas; and large central hearths.

Many homes even include a propped ladder, for decorative purposes.

Today's Pueblo homes are able to take full advantage of the Southwestern sun, however, and often include multiple windows and plenty of sliding doors that open to expansive porches. ■

Courtyards are a common element in Southwestern homes; this one is accessed through a charmingly rustic wooden gate.

SPANISH AND MISSION STYLES

Spanish Colonial Style at a Glance

- LOW-PITCHED, TILED ROOF
- ONE STORY
- THICK WALLS
- NARROW DOORS
- SMALL WINDOWS
- LARGE CENTRAL COURTYARDS

The earliest Spanish settlers often lived in remote colonial outposts, so their homes were simple and unadorned. Low-pitched, tiled roofs, and thick walls (composed of stucco over adobe bricks or stone) defined these one-story designs; for defense purposes, doors were narrow and windows were small. However, Spanish settlers who lived in cities and towns built more elaborate homes; these larger designs, although still one-story, were constructed around spacious central courtyards with portales, or covered porches. Each room of the home opened onto this central courtyard; usually, no interior doorways were included and people moved from one room to the other by crossing the courtyard. Inside, furnishings were sparse and handmade; the homes that did include interior doorways used heavy cloth instead of wooden doors to separate the rooms. Ceilings made of vigas and latillas prevailed in this design style as well.

Below: An expansive balcony, an outdoor staircase, and arched windows combine on the facade of this Spanish Eclectic home. Plan HPT810073, see page 126 for details

The Mission style, much more ornate and elaborate than early Spanish Colonial designs, originated in California in the early 1890s. Roofs, although still tiled, were higher-pitched and often hipped, and the smooth stucco facades featured more decorative elements, such as quatrefoil windows and curved parapets. Some architects even designed faithful reproductions of early religious missions, complete with ornamental bell towers.

The early 20th century brought Spanish Eclectic style to the forefront in the southwestern states. Like Mission-style homes, Spanish Eclectic homes are more complex than their simply decorated Colonial predecessors. They incorporate architectural details from the Spanish homes of the American Southwest, but they also include many of the elements of Spanish-style homes in Europe. Spanish Eclectic homes—often more than one story—showcase multilevel rooflines, sometimes with round or square towers. Exterior staircases allow for movement from level to level and usually access expansive covered porches and balconies as well. Decorative tiles frequently surround doors and pave interior courtyards, and wrought-iron grilles commonly cover windows (which are often full-length and arched). ■

Mission Style at a Glance

- SMOOTH WHITE STUCCO EXTERIOR
- HIGH-PITCHED, HIPPED ROOFLINES
- QUATREFOIL WINDOWS
- ORNATE PARAPETS
- DECORATIVE ELEMENTS LIKE FOUNTAINS AND BELL TOWERS
- USUALLY TWO OR MORE STORIES

Spanish Eclectic Style at a Glance

- USUALLY TWO OR MORE STORIES
- STUCCO EXTERIOR
- MULTILEVEL ROOFLINES
- ROUND OR SQUARE TOWERS
- EXTERIOR STAIRCASES
- COVERED PORCHES AND BALCONIES ON EACH STORY
- WROUGHT-IRON GRILLES OVER WINDOWS

Above: This classic Spanish Colonial design features a low-pitched tiled roof, an elegant entry courtyard, and wrought-iron accents. Plan HPT810086; see page 139 for details. Below: An ornate parapet, a smooth stucco facade, and two decorative bell towers define this plan as a Mission-style home. Plan HPT810029, see page 73 for details.

TERRITORIAL STYLE

Territorial Style at a Glance

- SYMMETRICAL EXTERIORS
- WOOD TRIM
- SHUTTERED WINDOWS
- THICK ADOBE WALLS
- LOW-PITCHED ROOFS COVERED IN CORRUGATED TIN
- FULL-LENGTH COVERED PORCHES

In the mid-1800s, the Greek Revival-style homes of the eastern states inspired people in the southwestern territories to create their own adaptations. These designs featured the symmetrical exteriors, wood trim, and shuttered windows of Greek Revival style combined with the thick adobe walls of other Southwestern homes. Roofs were low-pitched and covered in corrugated tin, and covered porches spanned the entire front of the home. ▪

Below: A standing-seam tin roof pairs with a stucco facade on this Territorial design, which also boasts a full-length covered front porch. Plan HPT810006; see page 50 for details.

CONTEMPORARY
SOUTHWESTERN PLANS

A wide variety of homes fills the Southwest today. In addition to the Pueblo, Spanish Colonial, Mission, and Territorial styles, many southwestern towns have their own unique looks. Residents of the Southwest came, and continue to arrive today, from all areas of the world, bringing their own ideas about architecture with them. Some small mining towns, such as Bisbee, Arizona, are filled with colorful Victorian-style homes. In other cities, such as Tucson, Arizona, older neighborhoods pair the low-pitched roofs and sturdy porch supports of Craftsman designs with

Above: Sharp edges and plenty of glass lend a high-tech feel to this contemporary plan. Plan HPT810003; see page 34 for details. Right: A smooth, earth-toned stucco exterior allows this plan to fit into any Southwestern neighborhood. Plan HPT810008; see page 52 for details.

© 2002 Donald A. Gardner, Inc.

Above: A wrought-iron gate, stone accents, and a standing-seam roof add rustic Western style to this contemporary home. Plan HPT810009; see page 53 for details. stucco exteriors. Some people choose to build organic-looking adobe homes, with gently curving lines and earth-toned exteriors, and others construct imposing high-tech homes with sharp edges and lots of glass—and, oddly enough, both of these styles appear equally at home in a desert landscape. If you're planning on building a home in the Southwest, there are plenty of options; take advantage of the region's colorful cultural and historical influences to find the perfect design for you. ■

Glossary

ADOBE: Mud bricks that have been dried in the sun, but not fired. Traditionally used on a home's exterior, these bricks are covered with a finish coat of plaster or stucco.

ALACENA: A cupboard, usually five or six feet tall, that is recessed into an adobe wall.

BANCO: A bench or built-in seat, often found to either side of a fireplace.

CANALE: A wood gutter or a drain spout. Typically made from a carved-out log, they project from the corners of an adobe home so water can be carried away from the house.

HORNO: An outdoor adobe oven used for baking bread.

LATILLAS: Small wood boards (or sometimes real cactus ribs) that are laid over rafters or beams, creating a lattice-like ceiling finish.

NICHOS: A functional niche carved into an adobe wall, often used to display art objects.

PEREDITA: A low wall between rooms that stops drafts and directs traffic, yet allows warm air to circulate overhead.

PORTALE: A covered porch.

SALTILLO TILES: Large, square, unglazed clay pavers made in Saltillo and other areas of Mexico. Usually red or dark orange, they're used primarily for flooring.

VIGA: A beam or rafter, typically an unfinished pine log with the bark removed. Vigas often project through adobe walls to the exterior of the home.

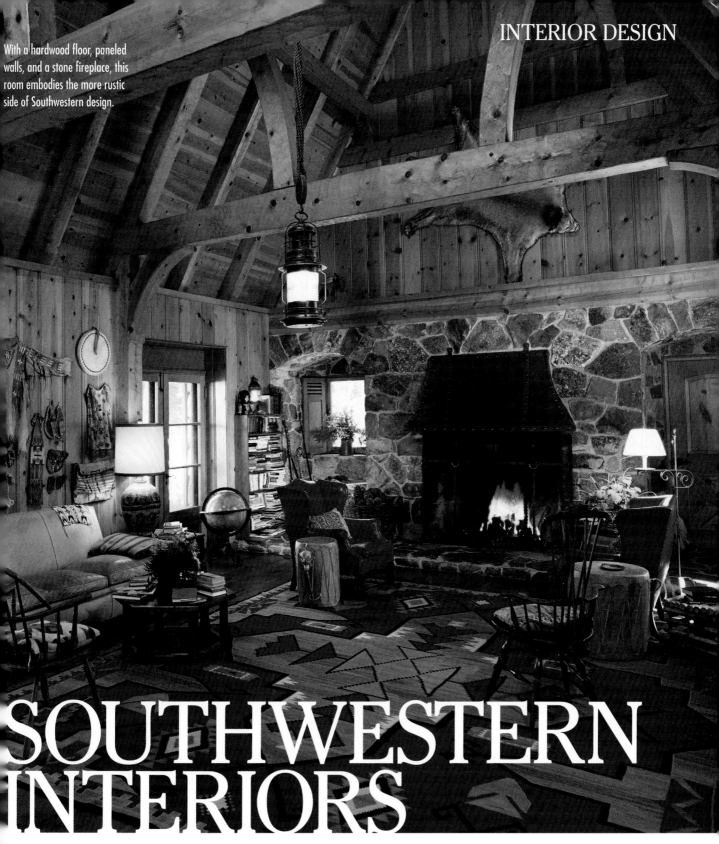

With a hardwood floor, paneled walls, and a stone fireplace, this room embodies the more rustic side of Southwestern design.

SOUTHWESTERN INTERIORS

ust like Southwestern architecture, Southwestern interior design ‌raws from a variety of cultural influences.

‌ addition to evoking the natural themes of Native American style and the religious motifs of ‌panish style, Southwestern interiors often integrate elements from other desert cultures: ‌exican, Moroccan, and even Turkish. This diversity allows plenty of freedom for those who wish ‌ incorporate Southwestern style into their homes.

INTERIOR DESIGN

They can choose a rustic style, with handcrafted furnishings, patterned woolen blankets, and hardwood walls and floors, or an ultramodern look, with expansive windows, neutral shades, and lots of natural light. Rooms can be made festive by incorporating the intense colors and themes of Mexican ceramic tiles, tapestries, and paintings—or soothing by including cool white and pastel shades. Furnishings and decorative accents are often an intriguing blend of antique and modern, and many pieces are handmade. Hundreds of artists and craftsmen find the Southwestern landscape inspirational; consequently, a wide assortment of unique furnishings and accents is available in Southwestern galleries and shops.

Looking to bring Southwestern style to your home? Find your inspiration in the following photo gallery, which showcases the many sides of Southwestern design—from the woven baskets and pottery of Native American style to the hardwood floors and rough-hewn furniture of rustic Southwestern style. ■

Right: A distinctive central hearth serves as the focal point of this gathering area, which also boasts a soaring ceiling, hardwood floor, and a unique blend of furnishings and accent pieces. Below: Fireplaces, both indoor and outdoor, are a common element in Southwestern homes; this indoor fireplace features a banco to the right. For more details, see Plan HPT810001 on page 25.

INTERIOR DESIGN

The same distinctive Southwestern tiles appear in the kitchen, master bedroom, and gathering area of this home. A variety of Western and Southwestern artwork — wrought iron and paintings in the gathering area, antique lanterns in the kitchen, and pottery in the bedroom — gives each room flair.

INTERIOR DESIGN

Right: Woven baskets, distinctive pottery, and patterned throw rugs serve as decorative elements in this Southwestern gathering room. For more details, see Plan HPT810001 on page 25. Below: A unique floor treatment, plenty of decorative ceramic tiles, and weathered cabinetry create a thoroughly rustic look in this Southwestern kitchen. For more details, see Plan HPT810001 on page 25. Opposite: Native American artwork and a ceiling that's composed of vigas and latillas combine to give this room authentic Southwestern style.

INTERIOR DESIGN

Above: Thick white walls, a corner fireplace, and sturdy vigas establish this room's Southwestern character. For more details, see Plan HPT810004 on page 39. Right: Skylights and a triple window bring the warm Southwestern sun to this bath. For more, see Plan HPT810002 on page 29.

Above: Natural woods lend warmth to the cool neutral and pastel shades of this bedroom, which is brightened by sunlight and two wall sconces. Left: Bright tiles, along with a niche above the fireplace, lend Spanish flair to this sitting area.

Above: A vivid, patterned carpet complements the hardwood floor in this bedroom, which includes a corner hearth. Right: A bed carved with Southwestern patterns is the centerpiece of this master suite. For more details, see Plan HPT810005 on page 44.

Natural earth tones help this classic Santa Fe home blend in with the environment.

CLASSIC SANTA FE

The rustic appeal of this spacious home exemplifies authentic Southwestern style and blends in with the surrounding desert landscape.

This charming design sits gracefully in the foothills of an Arizona mountain range. Vigas project through the inner walls to the home's exterior, creating an authentic Santa Fe look. A covered porch attached to the home's front facade, as well as a spacious rear terrace, add classic Southwestern style.

An expansive sunken gathering room serves as the heart of the comfortable floor plan. A raised hearth, built-in cabinetry topped by a bookshelf, and three separate entrances to the outdoors—one to the rear terrace and two more to the covered front porch—further enhance this room. The adjacent dining room also opens to the rear terrace.

A second hearth, this one with a built-in bench to the side, is found in the family kitchen area. Here, a nearby sitting area includes a built-in entertainment center. The main kitchen, with an L-shaped countertop, boasts an island cooktop/snack bar and a large pantry. A

Above: A banco, used here as a comfortable spot to enjoy the fire, sits to the side of this classic Southwestern-style hearth, which is further accented by decorative stencils and a small niche for wood storage. Left: A variety of Southwestern accents—pottery, ironwork, and woven baskets—fills the gathering room.

The home's terrace is the perfect spot to enjoy warm sunny days and cool desert nights.

built-in computer center and the utility area are found just around the corner.

The luxurious master suite resides to the left of the plan; here, a corner fireplace provides a Southwestern touch, and a well-appointed bath includes a corner whirlpool tub, separate shower, dual vanities, and a compartmented toilet. A walk-in closet offers plenty of space for clothing storage. Adjacent to the master suite is a charming guest suite with a full bath and access to a private covered porch. To the right of the plan, two additional bedrooms—one of which overlooks the terrace—share a full dual-vanity bath. ∎

plan# HPT810001

STYLE: SANTA FE
SQUARE FOOTAGE: 3,144
BEDROOMS: 4
BATHROOMS: 3
WIDTH: 139'-10"
DEPTH: 63'-8"
FOUNDATION: SLAB

SEARCH ONLINE @ EPLANS.COM

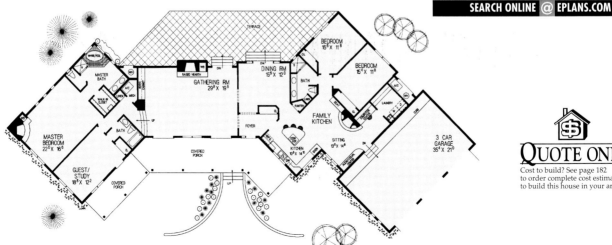

Quote One®
Cost to build? See page 182 to order complete cost estimate to build this house in your area!

ELEGANT HEIGHTS

High ceilings adorn this home's interior and the sloping lot enables the rear of the design to feature an expansive deck and terrace.

A tiled roof tops the striking white stucco exterior of this multilevel plan, creating a combination that will look at home in any landscape. Designed to fit a sloping lot, this home places the living quarters on the main floor but includes additional rooms and amenities on the lower level.

Perfect as either a coastal home or as a mountain retreat, this versatile three-bedroom plan would be a beautiful addition to any Southwestern neighborhood.

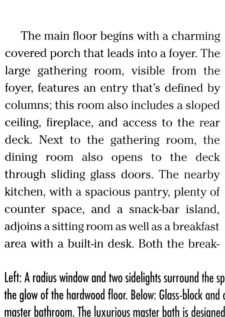

The main floor begins with a charming covered porch that leads into a foyer. The large gathering room, visible from the foyer, features an entry that's defined by columns; this room also includes a sloped ceiling, fireplace, and access to the rear deck. Next to the gathering room, the dining room also opens to the deck through sliding glass doors. The nearby kitchen, with a spacious pantry, plenty of counter space, and a snack-bar island, adjoins a sitting room as well as a breakfast area with a built-in desk. Both the break-fast and sitting rooms open to the deck. The laundry area, discreetly placed beyond the kitchen, includes two closets and a built-in counter; a powder room provides extra convenience.

The master suite dominates the left side of the plan. Two roomy walk-in closets, a dual vanity, a shower with a built-in seat, and a whirlpool tub surrounded by windows enhance the master bath. A media room, with a built-in entertainment center along one wall, adjoins the master suite.

Downstairs, a large activities room

Left: A radius window and two sidelights surround the spacious entry, bringing plenty of natural light to enhance the glow of the hardwood floor. Below: Glass-block and casement windows join two skylights in brightening the master bathroom. The luxurious master bath is designed to pamper the homeowner with its grand soaking tub.

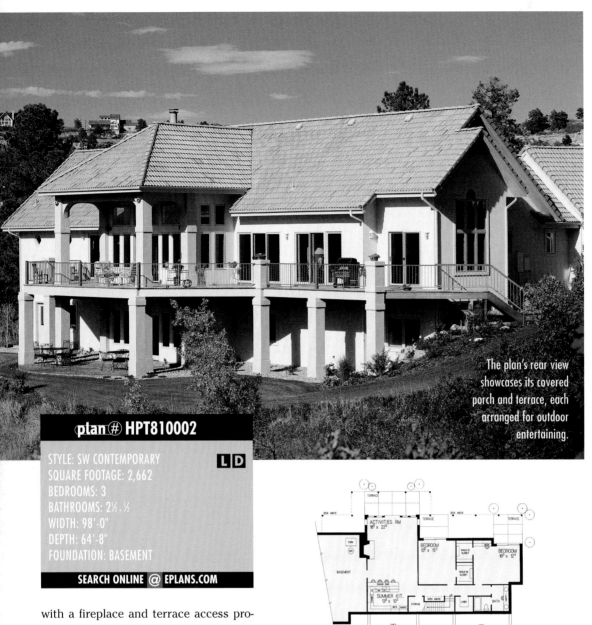

The plan's rear view showcases its covered porch and terrace, each arranged for outdoor entertaining.

plan# HPT810002

STYLE: SW CONTEMPORARY

L D

SQUARE FOOTAGE: 2,662
BEDROOMS: 3
BATHROOMS: 2½ + ½
WIDTH: 98'-0"
DEPTH: 64'-8"
FOUNDATION: BASEMENT

SEARCH ONLINE @ EPLANS.COM

with a fireplace and terrace access provides a great informal gathering spot; a summer kitchen, with a snack bar and pantry, makes hosting parties easy. Two additional bedrooms, both with walk-in closets and one with a built-in desk, share a full bath and open to the terrace. ■

QUOTE ONE®

Cost to build? See page 182 to order complete cost estimate to build this house in your area!

SECOND FLOOR

FIRST FLOOR

THIS HOME, AS SHOWN IN THE PHOTOGRAPHS, MAY DIFFER FROM THE ACTUAL BLUEPRINTS. FOR MORE DETAILED INFORMATION, PLEASE CHECK THE FLOOR PLANS CAREFULLY.

TO ORDER BLUEPRINTS CALL TOLL FREE 1-800-521-679

Marble countertops, sleek silver hanging lamps, and a mirrored wall lend a modern look to the kitchen.

LEARNING CURVE

This home boasts a unique contemporary design, evident everywhere from the seamless facade to the distinct interior.

Multiple windows and plenty of outdoor space make this contemporary design at home in a desert landscape. Inside, curved walls and unusually shaped rooms enhance the open floor plan. The circular living room, with an entry defined by columns, serves as the heart of the home. A curved wall of windows, divided by a raised-hearth fireplace, overlooks the expansive rear terrace. A built-in art display niche lines one wall of the living room; along the opposite wall, a sliding glass door opens to the covered porch. The formal dining room, just steps away from the living room, also boasts a curved window wall; a closet near the dining room allows for extra storage space.

Below: Topped by a transom, glass double doors open to a spectacular entryway in this contemporary home. Right: Glass-block windows to each side of the entry provide plenty of natural light in the main hallway, yet maintain privacy.

Above: The light-filled master suite appears even larger with high ceilings. It also includes plenty of space for a private sitting area, perfect for quiet conversation or an intimate breakfast. Right: This relaxing retreat is designed to pamper the home-owner. A whirlpool tub and glass-block windows accent the lavish master bath.

To the right of the living room, a trio of rooms—the kitchen, family room, and an eating nook—creates a casual family living space. The family room, with a second raised-hearth fireplace, includes sliding glass doors that open to both the terrace and the covered porch; the eating nook also opens to the outdoors. The kitchen boasts an efficient design,

with a double sink, a corner pantry, an a snack bar that overlooks the eatin nook and family room. The laundry are tucked discreetly behind the kitche opens to a full bath.

All four bedrooms offer luxuriou amenities. The first-floor master suit accessed by a long hallway, feature sliding glass doors that open to th

SECOND FLOOR

FIRST FLOOR

plan# HPT810003

L

STYLE: SW CONTEMPORARY
FIRST FLOOR: 2,422 SQ. FT.
SECOND FLOOR: 714 SQ. FT.
TOTAL: 3,136 SQ. FT.
BEDROOMS: 4
BATHROOMS: 4
WIDTH: 77'-6"
DEPTH: 62'-0"
FOUNDATION: SLAB

SEARCH ONLINE @ EPLANS.COM

QUOTE ONE®
Cost to build? See page 182
to order complete cost estimate
to build this house in your area!

terrace; its private bath includes two vanities, a walk-in closet, a whirlpool tub, and a compartmented toilet. A guest bedroom, also on the first floor, provides a walk-in closet and a private bath, and it opens to the front terrace. Upstairs, two more bedrooms, each with a walk-in closet, share a full bath and a balcony that overlooks the living room and foyer. ∎

Dramatic lighting, sleek black countertops, and a built-in desk give this kitchen a fully modern look.

SOUTHWEST STYLE

Santa Fe styling creates dramatic angles in this one-story home. The unique facade is architecturally stunning, yet at home in this rugged environment.

This sprawling Southwestern design, with a warm earth-toned exterior that blends well with the desert landscape, creates marvelous indoor/outdoor relationships. The plan opens with a spacious entry courtyard that's accessed through a wrought-iron gate. Just inside, an expansive skylight brightens the foyer, which includes a coat closet and a powder room. The centrally located living and dining rooms combine to create a lovely formal entertaining area. A three-sided fireplace—shared by the living and dining rooms as well as the covered rear porch—provides extra warmth. Each room offers sliding glass doors that open to the porch—a classic Southwestern portale that spans almost the full length of the home—and the living room boasts a beamed ceiling. An art niche sits to one side of the dining room's entry.

The Santa Fe style home blends in beautifully with the spectacular desert landscape. Vigas and cool stucco give the exterior added texture and Pueblo style, seamlessly linking the three-car garage with the rest of the home.

This living room showcases a multitude of Southwestern details: ceiling vigas, a corner fireplace accented by nichos, and easy access to the outdoors.

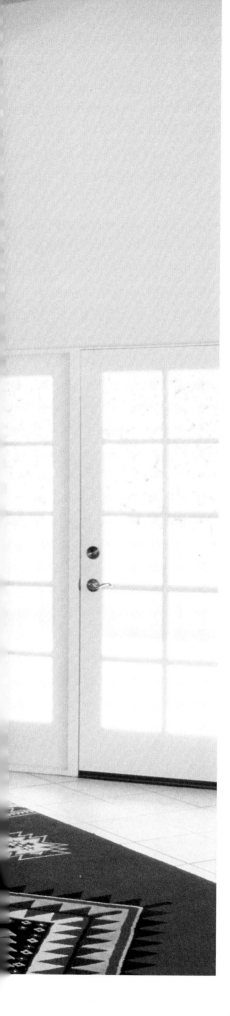

Vivid colors and soft lighting accent the master bedroom, where an elegant archway leads to the master bath.

The display niches found elsewhere in the home carry through even to the skillfully tiled master bath, creating a wonderful feeling of continuity.

FEATURED HOMES

The more casual family area, found to the left of the plan, consists of a cozy family room, kitchen, and breakfast area. The family room, which opens to the porch, includes a large storage closet along one wall. The kitchen, with a pantry and an island range, adjoins the breakfast area, which opens to a side porch. Just outside the kitchen, a short hallway leads to the laundry room, which opens to a side courtyard. Two nearby bedrooms, each with outdoor access, share a full dual-vanity bath that includes a linen closet and a whirlpool tub.

The amenity-filled master suite resides to the right of the plan; here, a private porch, a walk-in closet, and a bath with a whirlpool tub, separate shower, extra linen closet, and compartmented toilet create a relaxing sanctuary. Next to the master suite, a study with access to the covered front porch can double as a home office. ∎

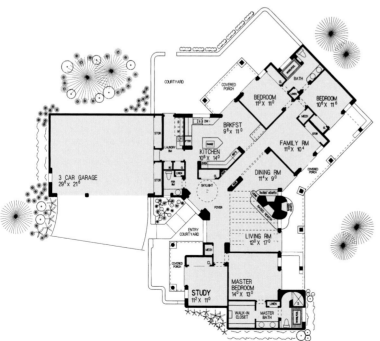

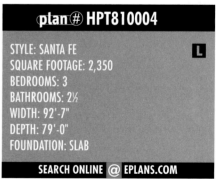

plan# HPT810004

STYLE: SANTA FE
SQUARE FOOTAGE: 2,350
BEDROOMS: 3
BATHROOMS: 2½
WIDTH: 92'-7"
DEPTH: 79'-0"
FOUNDATION: SLAB

SEARCH ONLINE @ EPLANS.COM

QUOTE ONE®
Cost to build? See page 182
to order complete cost estimate
to build this house in your area!

SOMEWHERE TO CALL HOME

In less than 3,000 square feet, this contemporary Southwestern home boasts five bedrooms and four full baths.

A red tile roof and a stucco exterior lend Southwestern flair to the clean lines of this contemporary design. Inside, the floor plan boasts amenities that are just as up-to-date as the exterior. To the right of the foyer, columns outline the entry of the living room, which includes a sloped ceiling and a bay window; an arched opening leads from the living room to the adjacent dining room. The study, located to the left of the foyer, includes built-in bookshelves; a nearby powder room allows this room to double as a guest suite.

Radius windows accent this home's front facade and are just one of the unique features found within. The space-savvy design includes a functional layout complete with a two-car garage, master suite, and outdoor patio.

Chairs in the kitchen and breakfast nook feature simple Southwestern carvings and patterns. A high-sloped ceiling makes these rooms appear even more spacious.

The kitchen/breakfast nook area is naturally illuminated by skylights and a bay window. A cozy niche in the nook provides a place to put a planning desk or store cookbooks. The L-shaped kitchen counter, with a convenient central cooktop, provides room for multiple cooks, and a pantry offers extra storage space. A snack bar overlooks the expansive family room, which boasts a sloped ceiling, a fireplace with a raised tile hearth, and a built-in entertainment center. A large rear patio, accessible from the family room, allows space for outdoor gatherings.

The master suite, shielded from street

Right: A bay window, topped by a radius window, brings plenty of natural light to the living room. Above: The foyer provides views of the living and dining rooms; note the column and the plant shelf that highlight the entry to the dining room.

Light-colored walls and a sloped ceiling add extra space to the simply decorated master bedroom.

plan# HPT810005

STYLE: SW CONTEMPORARY
FIRST FLOOR: 2,022
SECOND FLOOR: 845
TOTAL: 2,867
BEDROOMS: 5
BATHROOMS: 4
WIDTH: 63'-8"
DEPTH: 56'-2"
FOUNDATION: SLAB

SEARCH ONLINE @ EPLANS.COM

QUOTE ONE®
Cost to build? See page 182
to order complete cost estimate
to build this house in your area!

SECOND FLOOR

FIRST FLOOR

noise by the garage, sits to the rear of the plan; here, a bay window brightens the bedroom, and two walk-in closets ensure plenty of room for clothing storage. Special features in the elegant master bath include a dual vanity, a linen closet, and a whirlpool tub set under a window. Upstairs, three secondary bedrooms—one with a private bath and walk-in closet—share a loft/reading alcove that overlooks the family room. ∎

TO ORDER BLUEPRINTS CALL TOLL FREE 1-800-521-67

SOUTHWESTERN
SHOWCASE

This Welcoming Design Displays Pueblo and Santa Fe Influences. Plan HPT810017; see 61 for details.

SECOND FLOOR

FIRST FLOOR

Quote One®

Cost to build? See page 182
to order complete cost estimate
to build this house in your area!

plan# HPT810006

L

STYLE: TERRITORIAL
FIRST FLOOR: 3,166 SQ. FT.
SECOND FLOOR: 950 SQ. FT.
TOTAL: 4,116 SQ. FT.
BEDROOMS: 6
BATHROOMS: 5
WIDTH: 154'-0"
DEPTH: 94'-8"
FOUNDATION: SLAB

SEARCH ONLINE @ EPLANS.COM

A long low-pitched roof and a stucco
exterior distinguish this Territorial design. The
tiled entrance leads to a grand dining room and
opens to a formal parlor secluded by half-walls.
A country kitchen with a cooktop island overlooks the two-story gathering room with its full
wall of glass, fireplace and built-in media
shelves. The master suite satisfies the most dis-
cerning tastes with a raised hearth, an adjacent
study or exercise room, access to the wraparound porch, and a bath with corner whirlpool
tub. Rooms upstairs can serve as secondary
bedrooms for family members, be converted to
home office space or used as guest bedrooms.

TO ORDER BLUEPRINTS CALL TOLL FREE 1-800-521-679

plan# HPT810007

STYLE: SW CONTEMPORARY
SQUARE FOOTAGE: 3,505
BEDROOMS: 3
BATHROOMS: 2½
WIDTH: 110'-7"
DEPTH: 66'-11"
FOUNDATION: SLAB

SEARCH ONLINE @ EPLANS.COM

Loaded with custom features, this plan is designed to delight the imagination. The foyer enters directly into the commanding sunken gathering room. Framed by an elegant railing, this centerpiece for entertaining is open to both the study and the formal dining room, and offers sliding glass doors to the terrace. A full bar further extends the entertaining possibilities of this room. The country-style kitchen contains an efficient work area, as well as a morning room and sitting area—ideal for family gatherings around the cozy fireplace. The grand master suite has a private terrace, fireplace alcove with built-in seats and a huge spa-style bath. Two nicely sized bedrooms and hall bath round out the plan.

QUOTE ONE®
Cost to build? See page 182
to order complete cost estimate
to build this house in your area!

plan⊕ HPT810008

STYLE: SW CONTEMPORARY
SQUARE FOOTAGE: 1,746
BEDROOMS: 3
BATHROOMS: 2
WIDTH: 58'-0"
DEPTH: 59'-4"
FOUNDATION: SLAB

SEARCH ONLINE @ EPLANS.COM

Wooden window accents bring a rustic flavor to this warm Southwestern design. Double doors open to the foyer: to the right, a vaulted dining room is enhanced by bright multi-pane windows. The study opens to the left through stylish French doors. Ahead, the vaulted great room ushers in natural light. An efficient kitchen easily serves the bayed breakfast nook for simple casual meals. Two family bedrooms share a full bath, creating a quiet zone for the master suite. A corner whirlpool tub, oversized walk-in closet, and sliding-glass-door lanai access make this retreat a true haven.

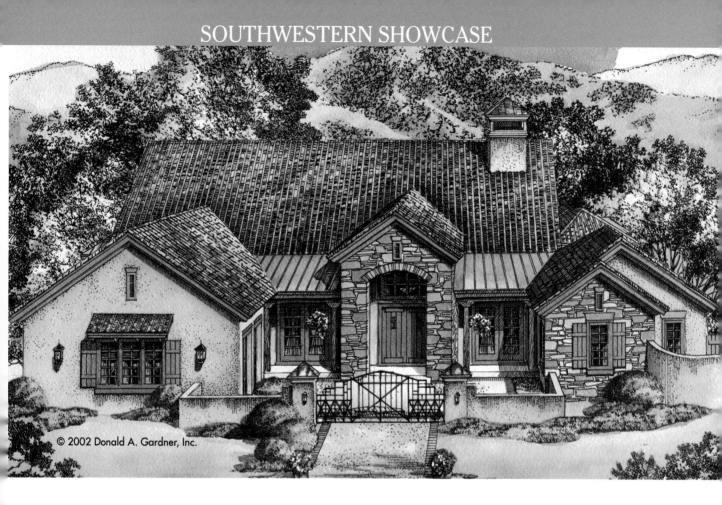

plan⊞ HPT810009

STYLE: SW CONTEMPORARY
SQUARE FOOTAGE: 3,061
BEDROOMS: 3
BATHROOMS: 3½
WIDTH: 86'-1"
DEPTH: 84'-8"

SEARCH ONLINE @ EPLANS.COM

Meanwhile, back at the ranch...an updated hacienda was offering the utmost in livability. Enter through a rugged stone lanai to an elegant gallery hall, which accesses the combined great room/dining area. A double-sided fireplace warms this space as well as the courtyard to the right. The adjacent master suite features a curved wall of windows and a deluxe bath with a huge walk-in closet. On the opposite side of the plan, the kitchen's serving-bar island looks into the bay-windowed breakfast nook. A roomy pantry will delight the family cook. Opening from the other side of the kitchen is a hearth-warmed family room that accesses the rear lanai. At the right front of the plan reside two additional bedrooms—each with its own bath.

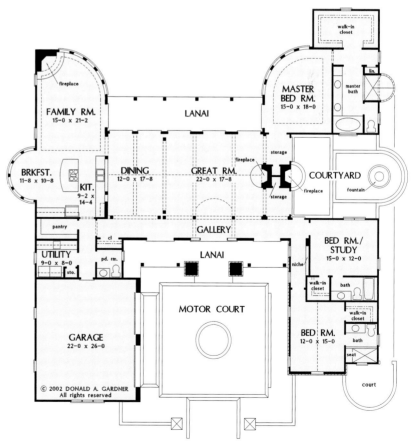

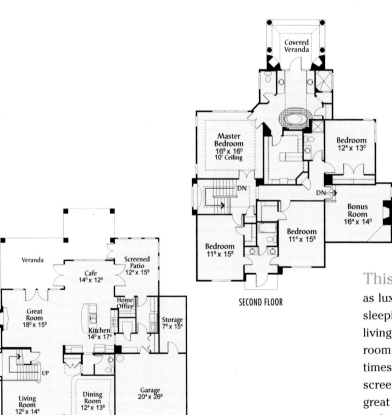

Covered Veranda

Master Bedroom
16⁸ x 16⁰
10' Ceiling

Bedroom
12⁴ x 13⁰

DN

DN

Bonus Room
16⁴ x 14⁰

Bedroom
11⁴ x 15⁸

Bedroom
11⁸ x 15⁸

SECOND FLOOR

Veranda

Cafe
14⁰ x 12⁰

Screened Patio
12⁴ x 15⁸

Great Room
18⁰ x 15⁸

Home Office

Kitchen
14⁰ x 17⁴

Storage
7⁸ x 15⁴

UP

Living Room
12⁰ x 14⁴

Dining Room
12⁴ x 13⁸

Garage
20⁴ x 26⁸

Cvr'd Porch

Courtyard

FIRST FLOOR

plan⊞ HPT810010

STYLE: SW CONTEMPORARY
FIRST FLOOR: 1,596 SQ. FT.
SECOND FLOOR: 1,619 SQ. FT.
TOTAL: 3,215 SQ. FT.
BONUS SPACE: 238 SQ. FT.
BEDROOMS: 4
BATHROOMS: 3½
WIDTH: 55'-4"
DEPTH: 76'-4"
FOUNDATION: SLAB

SEARCH ONLINE @ EPLANS.COM

This contemporary design is thoughtful as well as luxurious, placing living spaces on the first floor and sleeping quarters upstairs. On the first floor, a spacious living/dining area sits just beyond the entry. The great room, kitchen and cafe area—perfect for more casual times—all have easy access to a covered rear veranda. A screened patio, accessible from the cafe area, provides a great place for outdoor dining. A petite home office is tucked discreetly to the side of the kitchen. Upstairs, three family bedrooms—two with walk-in closets—join the master suite. Here, the expansive master bath opens to a covered veranda with two fireplaces. A bonus room, also with a fireplace, can serve as a family gathering area.

TO ORDER BLUEPRINTS CALL TOLL FREE 1-800-521-679

plan# HPT810011

STYLE: SW CONTEMPORARY
FIRST FLOOR: 1,324 SQ. FT.
SECOND FLOOR: 1,081 SQ. FT.
TOTAL: 2,405 SQ. FT.
BEDROOMS: 5
BATHROOMS: 2½
WIDTH: 49'-4"
DEPTH: 61'-0"
FOUNDATION: BASEMENT

SEARCH ONLINE @ EPLANS.COM

This five-bedroom contemporary design features a stunning array of special amenities. Two fireplaces—in the great and hearth rooms—enhance the first floor. Upstairs, the private master-suite veranda and a shared front veranda each boast a fireplace as well. The dining room, cafe area, great room and hearth room all offer access to the rear patio, and the study provides French doors that open to the front courtyard. The gourmet island kitchen contains space for multiple cooks. A large walk-in closet and a splendid bath with a spa tub highlight the master suite.

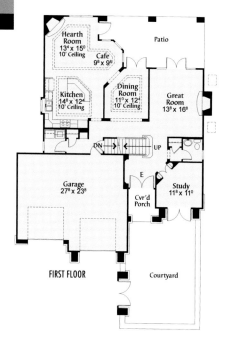

FIRST FLOOR

SECOND FLOOR

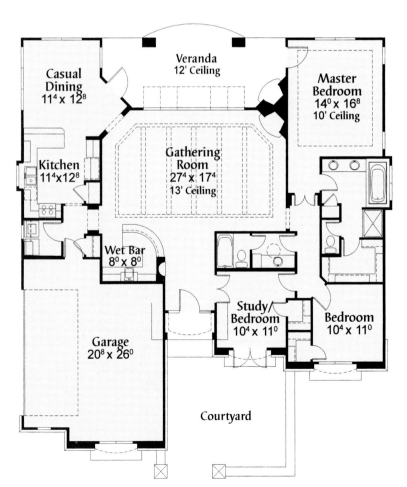

plan# HPT810012

STYLE: SW CONTEMPORARY
SQUARE FOOTAGE: 1,923
BEDROOMS: 3
BATHROOMS: 2
WIDTH: 55'-8"
DEPTH: 62'-8"
FOUNDATION: SLAB

SEARCH ONLINE @ EPLANS.COM

Bold rooflines announce the glass-door entrance of this contemporary design. The foyer opens directly to a gathering room with a thirteen-foot ceiling and corner fireplace. A nearby wet bar is great for guests. The kitchen easily serves the sunlit dining area, which opens to the rear veranda (with a fireplace!). Family bedrooms reside to the right and include a comfortable master suite with a private bath, and two secondary bedrooms. One bedroom also makes a fine study.

TO ORDER BLUEPRINTS CALL TOLL FREE 1-800-521-679

plan # HPT810013

STYLE: SW CONTEMPORARY
FIRST FLOOR: 2,260 SQ. FT.
SECOND FLOOR: 1,020 SQ. FT.
TOTAL: 3,280 SQ. FT.
BEDROOMS: 4
BATHROOMS: 2½
WIDTH: 69'-6"
DEPTH: 88'-2"
FOUNDATION: BASEMENT

SEARCH ONLINE @ EPLANS.COM

SECOND FLOOR

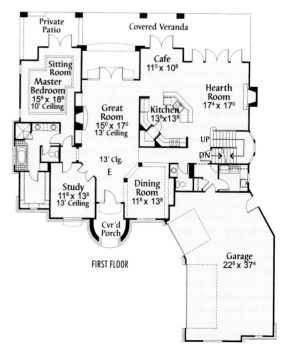

FIRST FLOOR

Multiple rooflines and a charming balcony give this contemporary design a hint of historic Spanish Colonial style, but the interior is completely in step with modern lifestyles. To the left of the foyer, double doors open to a study; to the right, decorative columns define the entrance to the formal dining room. The great room, with a fireplace, built-in shelves, and French doors that open to the covered rear veranda, provides a great informal gathering spot; another comfortable area is the hearth room, also with a fireplace and outdoor access. The master suite, with a sitting room and private patio, is secluded on the first floor. Upstairs, three additional bedrooms—all with walk-in closets—adjoin a home office with built-in cabinetry.

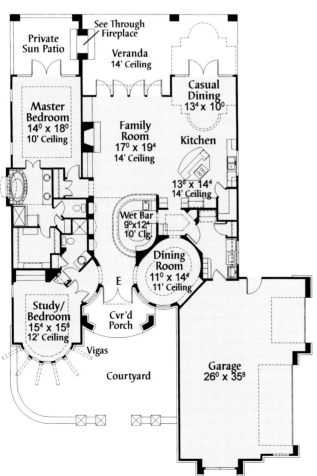

plan# HPT810014

STYLE: PUEBLO
SQUARE FOOTAGE: 2,126
BEDROOMS: 2
BATHROOMS: 2
WIDTH: 62'-8"
DEPTH: 79'-4"
FOUNDATION: SLAB

SEARCH ONLINE @ EPLANS.COM

This intriguing stucco pueblo is a modern tak on Southwestern style. On the exterior, canopied vig shade tall windows from the desert sun. Inside, thoughtf touches—art niches, natural lighting and extra-high cei ings—create a personalized appeal. Soffits light the glas door entry; on the right, an oval dining room with a nich makes an elegant statement. Just ahead, a full rounde wet bar is wonderful for entertaining. The kitchen equipped with a cooktop-island serving bar that ove looks the family room fireplace and bright casual dini area. The master bedroom awes with a sumptuous ba and private sun patio with a see-through fireplace.

plan # HPT810015

STYLE: SANTA FE
SQUARE FOOTAGE: 2,000
BEDROOMS: 3
BATHROOMS: 2½
WIDTH: 75'-0"
DEPTH: 55'-0"
FOUNDATION: SLAB

SEARCH ONLINE @ EPLANS.COM

QUOTE ONE®

Cost to build? See page 182
to order complete cost estimate
to build this house in your area!

This classic stucco design provides a cool retreat in any climate. From the covered porch, enter the skylit foyer to find an arched ceiling leading to the central gathering room with its raised-hearth fireplace and terrace access. A connecting corner dining room is conveniently located near the amenity-filled kitchen. The large master suite includes terrace access and a private bath with a whirlpool tub, a separate shower and plenty of closet space. A second bedroom and a study that can be converted to a bedroom complete this wonderful plan.

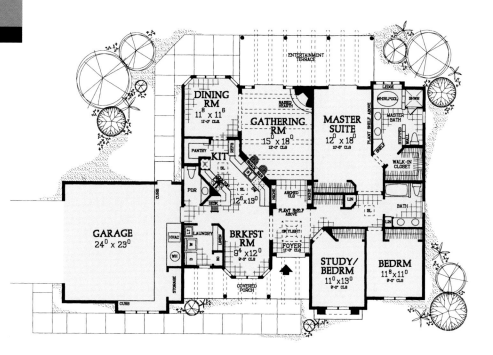

© 2002 Donald A. Gardner, Inc.

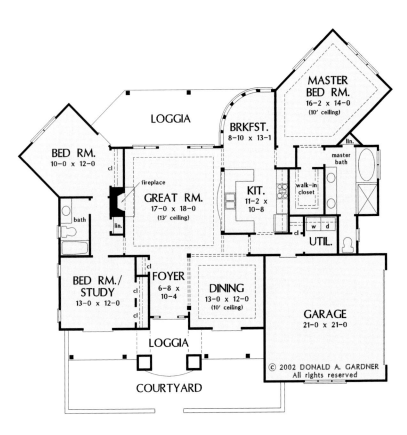

plan⊕ HPT810016

STYLE: SANTA FE
SQUARE FOOTAGE: 1,895
BEDROOMS: 3
BATHROOMS: 2
WIDTH: 65'-10"
DEPTH: 59'-9"

SEARCH ONLINE @ EPLANS.COM

Santa Fe style at its best brings you back t
the days of open skies and covered wagons. Ric
with history on the outside, this plan's interior ha
all the up-to-date amenities that today's familie
require. The arched loggia entry opens to a soarin
foyer, flanked on the right by a formal dining roon
To the left is a bedroom that could easily become
study. Straight ahead, the hearth-warmed grea
room enjoys sliding glass door access to the rea
loggia. Another bedroom is tucked in the back le
corner. On the other side of the great room, a room
kitchen opens to a breakfast nook with a curve
wall of windows. Secluded to the back is the lux
rious master suite, featuring a ten-foot ceiling an
spectacular private bath.

TO ORDER BLUEPRINTS CALL TOLL FREE 1-800-521-67

plan# HPT810017

STYLE: SANTA FE
SQUARE FOOTAGE: 3,343
BEDROOMS: 3
BATHROOMS: 2½ + ½
WIDTH: 84'-0"
DEPTH: 92'-0"
FOUNDATION: SLAB

SEARCH ONLINE @ EPLANS.COM

This distinctive stucco home is reminiscent of early Santa Fe-style architecture. Decorative vigas line the entry as double doors lead into an elongated columned foyer. A living/dining room combination ahead enjoys abundant light from three French doors, and the warmth of a Southwestern fireplace. An abbreviated hall leads either to the bedroom gallery or to the gourmet kitchen. A sunny nook and leisure room just beyond are bathed in natural light. A veranda grill is perfect in any season. Separated from the rest of the home for complete privacy, the master suite relishes a bay window, veranda access and a lavish bath.

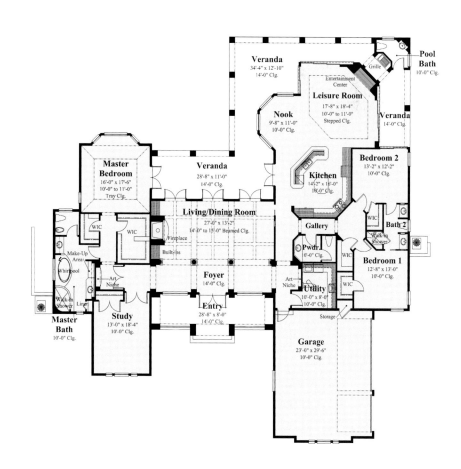

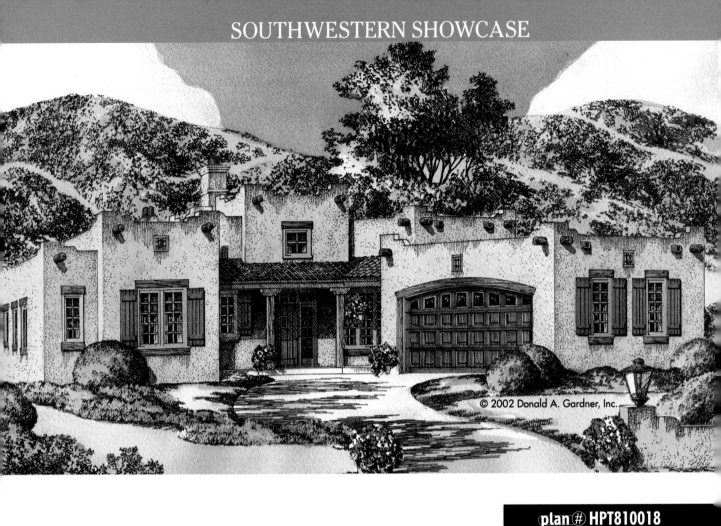

© 2002 Donald A. Gardner, Inc.

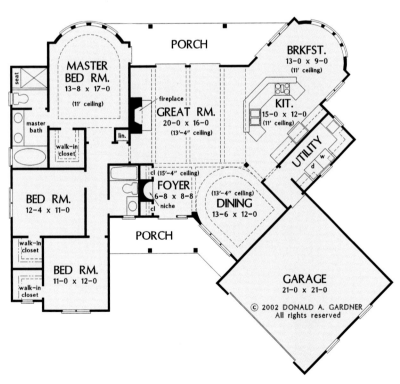

PORCH

MASTER BED RM.
13-8 x 17-0
(11' ceiling)

seat

master bath

walk-in closet

BED RM.
12-4 x 11-0

walk-in closet

BED RM.
11-0 x 12-0

walk-in closet

PORCH

fireplace

lin.

GREAT RM.
20-0 x 16-0
(13'-4" ceiling)

(15'-4" ceiling)

cl

FOYER
6-8 x 8-8

niche

cl

DINING
13-6 x 12-0
(13'-4" ceiling)

BRKFST.
13-0 x 9-0
(11' ceiling)

KIT.
15-0 x 12-0
(11' ceiling)

UTILITY

d w

GARAGE
21-0 x 21-0

© 2002 DONALD A. GARDNER
All rights reserved

plan# HPT810018

STYLE: SANTA FE
SQUARE FOOTAGE: 1,883
BEDROOMS: 3
BATHROOMS: 2
WIDTH: 66'-2"
DEPTH: 59'-8"

SEARCH ONLINE @ EPLANS.COM

Home on the range—where luxury and livability go hand-in-hand. Rustic details like heavy shutters and beams accent the facade of thi Santa Fe classic. Enter the front covered porc to the spacious foyer, which opens at a uniqu angle to the windowed formal dining room t the right. At the center of the home is th hearth-warmed great room, which flows righ into the island serving-bar kitchen and baye breakfast nook—both feature eleven-foot ce ings. The left wing of the plan is taken up by th sleeping quarters, including two family be rooms—each with its own walk-in closet—and deluxe master suite. The suite boasts anoth curved wall of windows, a walk-in closet, twi vanity bath and rear-porch access.

TO ORDER BLUEPRINTS CALL TOLL FREE 1-800-521-67

© 2002 Donald A. Gardner, Inc.

plan⊕ HPT810019

STYLE: SANTA FE
SQUARE FOOTAGE: 2,792
BEDROOMS: 3
BATHROOMS: 2½
WIDTH: 89'-2"
DEPTH: 88'-9

SEARCH ONLINE @ EPLANS.COM

ngles and arcs are intriguingly jux-
posed in this innovative new Santa Fe
esign. A Spanish-turret entry presents
he formal foyer and quiet study. In the
reat room, a cathedral ceiling soars.
he half-moon fireplace completes its
rcle in the sumptuous master suite; the
tting room benefits from circumam-
ent light. The left wing comprises a
ourmet island kitchen, bayed dining
om, and generous twin bedrooms. Not
be missed: a side-entry mudroom, and
fireplace on the rear porch.

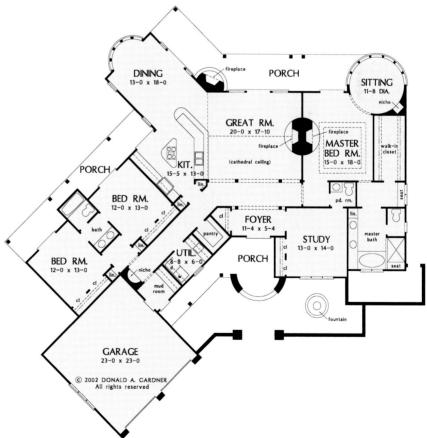

© The Sater Design Collection, Inc.

With a Spanish tile roof and a stucco exterior, this estate home holds the best of the Southwest. Upon entry, the foyer opens up to the living room and dining room combination, a highly requested feature in today's homes. A two-sided fireplace here shares its warmth with the study/library. The gourmet kitchen maximizes work space with wraparound countertops and an oversize island. The leisure room will be a family favorite, with a built-in entertainment center and outdoor access. Don't miss the outdoor grill and cabana suite on the far right. The master retreat is aptly named; a unique shape allows for an angled bath with a whirlpool tub and twin walk-in closets. Three additional bedrooms with private baths share two sun porches and convenient utility space.

plan⊕ HPT810020

STYLE: SPANISH COLONIAL
FIRST FLOOR: 1,995 SQ. FT.
SECOND FLOOR: 2,165 SQ. FT.
TOTAL: 4,160 SQ. FT.
BEDROOMS: 5
BATHROOMS: 5½
WIDTH: 58'-0"
DEPTH: 65'-0"
FOUNDATION: SLAB

SEARCH ONLINE @ EPLANS.COM

FIRST FLOOR

SECOND FLOOR

TO ORDER BLUEPRINTS CALL TOLL FREE 1-800-521-67

plan# HPT810021

STYLE: SW CONTEMPORARY
SQUARE FOOTAGE: 3,105
BEDROOMS: 4
BATHROOMS: 3½
WIDTH: 66'-0"
DEPTH: 91'-8"

SEARCH ONLINE @ EPLANS.COM

panish allure lends a magnificent quality to this southwestern design. An inviting foyer leads to a formal dining room on the left and beamed-ceiling study on the right. Ahead, a unique ceiling treatment defines the living room. An oversized island and space for a six-burner range create divine haute cuisine in no time. An outdoor grill is great in any season. From the leisure room, enter the nearby guest suite or follow sliding glass doors to the veranda. The outstanding master suite opens through French doors: on the left, the bedroom includes outdoor access. To the right, walk-in closets and a whirlpool bath view the privacy garden.

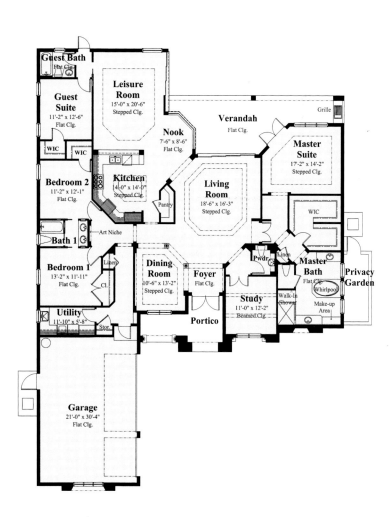

SECOND FLOOR

FIRST FLOOR

plan# HPT810022

STYLE: SW CONTEMPORARY
FIRST FLOOR: 3,556 SQ. FT.
SECOND FLOOR: 1,308 SQ. FT.
TOTAL: 4,864 SQ. FT.
BEDROOMS: 4
BATHROOMS: 3½
WIDTH: 95'-0"
DEPTH: 84'-8"
FOUNDATION: SLAB

SEARCH ONLINE @ EPLANS.COM

This Southwestern luxury home hosts over 1,00 square feet of outdoor living space, including private ba conies on two of the bedrooms. Although the Mediterranea inspired facade of this home will be the envy of you neighborhood, the true glory of the design is the brilliant floo plan inside. The foyer ushers guests into a bayed living roo with three sets of French doors. A two-way fireplace share with the study is a cozy touch. A vast country kitchen effor lessly serves the elegant dining room and cheerful nook. A re leisure room is awash with light, making it the perfect place f casual relaxation. If complete pampering is what you crav look no further than the master suite, with abundant natur light and a lavish whirlpool bath. The plan is completed three upper-level bedrooms and a loft overlook.

plan# HPT810023

STYLE: SW CONTEMPORARY
SQUARE FOOTAGE: 3,790
BEDROOMS: 4
BATHROOMS: 3½
WIDTH: 80'-0"
DEPTH: 107'-8"
FOUNDATION: SLAB

SEARCH ONLINE @ EPLANS.COM

A majestic desert oasis, this well-planned home puts family comfort and privacy first. Enter under a keystone portico to the foyer; a dramatic dining room opens to the right. Just ahead, the living room is an inviting place to relax by the fireplace. A unique kitchen supports gourmet meals, or a quick snack enjoyed in the sunny nook. An entertainment center separates the leisure room and game room—or finish the space to include a fourth bedroom. The rear guest suite offers a private bath and access to the veranda, featuring an outdoor grill. For the ultimate in luxury, the master suite is peerless; a light-filled sitting area, angled bedroom and indulgent bath make an inviting retreat for any homeowner

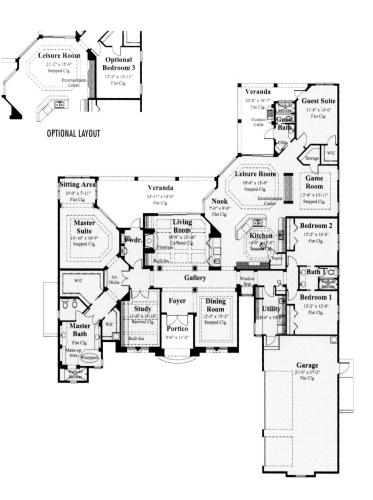

OPTIONAL LAYOUT

Mediterranean influences grace the exterior of this contemporary Southwestern home. Enter past a grand portico to the sunburst-lit foyer; a study and dining room to either side both enjoy stepped ceilings and French doors. A convenient butler's pantry leads from the dining room to the exquisitely appointed kitchen. A sunny bayed nook lies between the living room, with a built-in entertainment center, and a leisure room. Three nearby bedrooms share two full baths. The right wing is entirely devoted to the master suite. Here, the comfortable bedroom accesses the rear lanai; for pure luxury, the private bath features an extravagant whirlpool tub and walk-in shower. A three-car garage completes the plan.

plan# HPT810024

STYLE: SW CONTEMPORARY
SQUARE FOOTAGE: 2,908
BEDROOMS: 4
BATHROOMS: 3
WIDTH: 80'-10"
DEPTH: 59'-10"
FOUNDATION: SLAB

SEARCH ONLINE @ EPLANS.COM

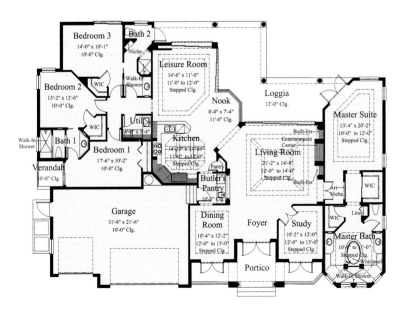

TO ORDER BLUEPRINTS CALL TOLL FREE 1-800-521-67

plan# HPT810025

STYLE: SW CONTEMPORARY
SQUARE FOOTAGE: 3,368
BEDROOMS: 3
BATHROOMS: 3½
WIDTH: 121'-5"
DEPTH: 99'-6"
FOUNDATION: SLAB

SEARCH ONLINE @ EPLANS.COM

Uniquely shaped rooms and luxurious amenities are the hallmark of this contemporary Southwestern design, which moves easily from indoors to outdoors. A large central foyer opens to formal rooms—study, living room and dining room. A hallway to the right of the foyer leads to informal areas—the kitchen, breakfast nook and leisure room. Two bedrooms, both with access to a spacious rear veranda, also reside in the right wing. The master suite, accessed by double doors and its own foyer, includes two walk-in closets, a lavish bath with a whirlpool tub, and a private garden.

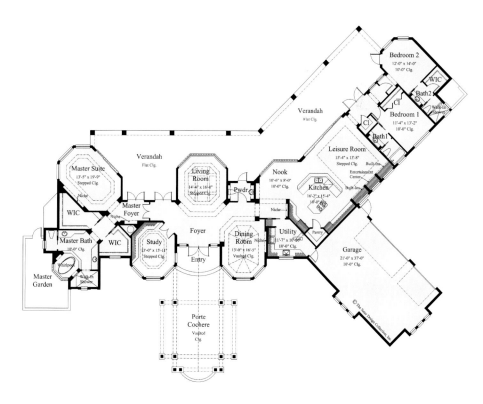

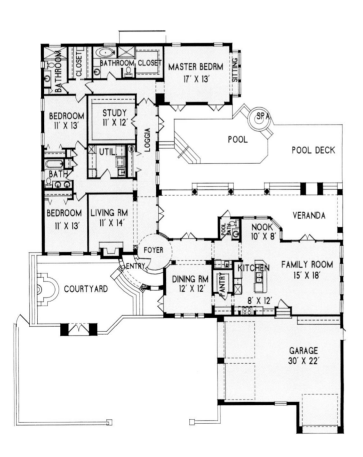

plan⊕ HPT810026

STYLE: SPANISH COLONIAL
SQUARE FOOTAGE: 2,892
BEDROOMS: 3
BATHROOMS: 3½
WIDTH: 84'-8"
DEPTH: 96'-8"
FOUNDATION: SLAB

SEARCH ONLINE @ EPLANS.COM

In an intriguing blend of Mediterranean and Mission styles, this captivating home exemplifie Spanish Colonial design. A gated entry leads to th courtyard, where a grand foyer awaits. To th right, a formal dining room with courtyard acces flows past the butler's pantry into an open vill kitchen. Both the family room and breakfast noo afford spectacular views through their walls windows. A pool bath is an added convenienc The left wing comprises a living room with a fir place, two secondary bedrooms, two full ha baths, a study and the utility room. To the rear, th master suite features a windowed sitting area, lu urious bath and outdoor access.

plan# HPT810027

STYLE: SPANISH COLONIAL
FIRST FLOOR: 2,828 SQ. FT.
SECOND FLOOR: 493 SQ. FT.
TOTAL: 3,321 SQ. FT.
BEDROOMS: 3
BATHROOMS: 3½
WIDTH: 80'-0"
DEPTH: 106'-2"
FOUNDATION: SLAB

SEARCH ONLINE @ EPLANS.COM

Beautiful exterior details and subtle Southwestern style make this home the hallmark of any neighborhood. Choose from three front-deck entries—two sets of French doors or a single foyer door—to find a lovely dining room, accessing a side courtyard. Continue to the great room, warmed by a fireplace, or the prominent island kitchen; both areas easily access the wet bar. The rear art room is well-lit for the burgeoning artist. The bayed master suite is a private sanctuary, embellished with a pampering bath and veranda access. Two family bedrooms—one to the front of the home and one upstairs—enjoy private baths.

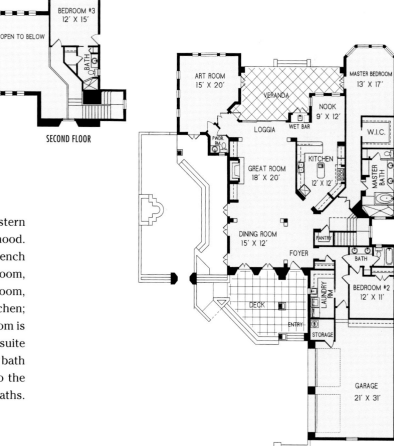

SECOND FLOOR

FIRST FLOOR

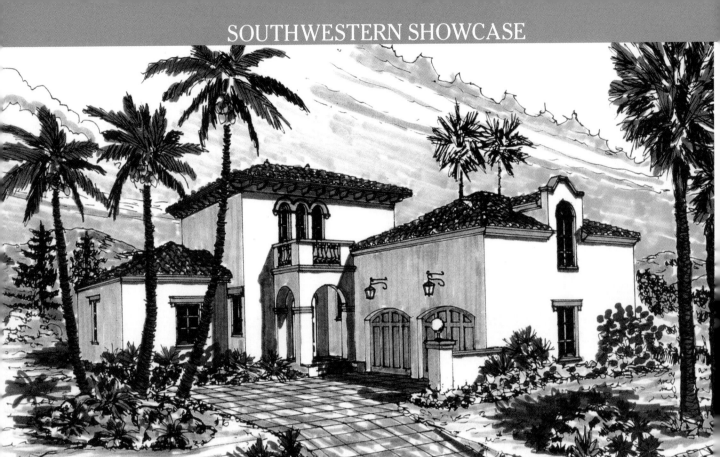

BEDROOM
12' X 10'

BEDROOM
12' X 10'

BATH

SECOND FLOOR

FUTURE
BONUS ROOM
17' X 18'

MASTER
BEDROOM
13' x 17'

VERANDA

GREAT ROOM
18' x 15'

DINING RM
11' x 14'

MASTER
BATH

FOYER

KITCHEN
10' x 10'

ENTRY

STORAGE

GARAGE
21' x 21'

FIRST FLOOR

plan# HPT810028

STYLE: SPANISH COLONIAL
FIRST FLOOR: 1,364 SQ. FT.
SECOND FLOOR: 462 SQ. FT.
TOTAL: 1,826 SQ. FT.
BONUS SPACE: 354 SQ. FT.
BEDROOMS: 3
BATHROOMS: 2½
WIDTH: 48'-8"
DEPTH: 69'-0"
FOUNDATION: SLAB

SEARCH ONLINE @ EPLANS.COM

With alluring detail and a strikin
Spanish tile roof, this historic home can b
surprisingly economical to build. Ente
under a pediment to find the great room
bathed in natural light. To the right,
sunny dining area flows into the angle
serving-bar kitchen for ultimate conven
ience. The first-floor master suite include
a box-bay sitting area and a splendid bat
with a spa tub. Upstairs, two bedroom
share a full bath. Bonus space above th
garage can be used as a study, game room
home gym—whatever your family desire

plan# HPT810029

STYLE: SPANISH COLONIAL
FIRST FLOOR: 3,788 SQ. FT.
SECOND FLOOR: 850 SQ. FT.
TOTAL: 4,638 SQ. FT.
BEDROOMS: 3
BATHROOMS: 4½
WIDTH: 103'-0"
DEPTH: 91'-0"
FOUNDATION: SLAB

SEARCH ONLINE @ EPLANS.COM

Designed for the family that values luxury as much as outdoor living, this Spanish Colonial villa employs an inspiring floor plan for a home like no other. Enter by way of an elaborate courtyard to an elongated foyer. To the right, luxurious sleeping quarters include two family suites and a master retreat with a lush bath and vast walk-in closet. The master bedroom and foyer access the coffered-ceiling study, which shares the warmth of its fireplace with the living room. The dining room flows effortlessly into the island kitchen. A rustic exposed-beam ceiling continues into the family room, complete with a corner fireplace. All living areas have veranda access. Upstairs, a game room and loft provide great places to unwind and have fun.

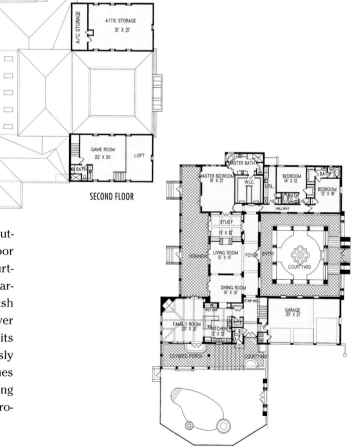

SECOND FLOOR

FIRST FLOOR

A striking Spanish Colonial facade, with tall, narrow windows and a charming balcony, introduces a home with an efficient modern floor plan. Inside, the large kitchen with a cooktop island easily serves the cozy family room and the formal dining/living area. A long gallery gives access to a half bath and laundry. The bedrooms are all upstairs, including the spacious master suite with walk-in closet and luxurious bath. Across the hall, two secondary bedrooms share a full bath.

plan# HPT810030

STYLE: SPANISH COLONIAL
FIRST FLOOR: 1,114 SQ. FT.
SECOND FLOOR: 959 SQ. FT.
TOTAL: 2,073 SQ. FT.
BEDROOMS: 3
BATHROOMS: 2½
WIDTH: 40'-0"
DEPTH: 60'-0"
FOUNDATION: SLAB

SEARCH ONLINE @ EPLANS.COM

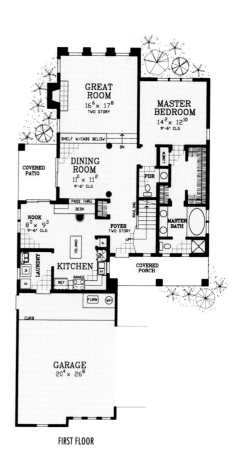

plan# HPT810031

STYLE: SPANISH COLONIAL
FIRST FLOOR: 1,473 SQ. FT.
SECOND FLOOR: 752 SQ. FT.
TOTAL: 2,225 SQ. FT.
BEDROOMS: 4
BATHROOMS: 2½
WIDTH: 40'-0"
DEPTH: 76'-6"
FOUNDATION: SLAB

SEARCH ONLINE @ EPLANS.COM

This compact Spanish-style home is enhanced by a gracefully arched front porch. The two-story foyer opens to the island kitchen and the formal dining room. The breakfast nook, adjacent to the kitchen, opens to a covered rear patio. A few steps down, the great room boasts a fireplace and a soaring two-story ceiling. The master bedroom is on the first floor, with a dressing area and a bath with His and Hers vanities. Upstairs, three family bedrooms share a full bath.

SECOND FLOOR

FIRST FLOOR

FIRST FLOOR

FAMILY 12⁰ × 16⁴ 9'-6" CLG

KITCHEN 13⁶ × 15¹⁰ 9'-6" CLG

COVERED PATIO

DINING 12⁰ × 9⁴ 9'-6" CLG

GALLERY 8'-6" CLG

LAUNDRY 6⁶ × 9⁸ 8'-6" CLG

ENTRY

LIVING 12⁰ × 14⁴ 9'-6" CLG

PDR

COVERED PORCH

GARAGE 21¹⁰ × 25⁰

SECOND FLOOR

BEDRM 3 12⁰ × 9⁶

FLEX ROOM 14⁴ × 12⁶

MASTER BATH

WET BAR

BATH

LINEN

STORAGE

WALK IN CLOSET

HALF WALL

OPEN TO BELOW

MASTER BEDRM 12⁰ × 15⁴

BEDRM 2 12⁰ × 10⁶

RAILING

plan# HPT810032

STYLE: SPANISH COLONIAL
FIRST FLOOR: 1,115 SQ. FT.
SECOND FLOOR: 1,188 SQ. FT.
TOTAL: 2,303 SQ. FT.
BEDROOMS: 3
BATHROOMS: 2½
WIDTH: 42'-0"
DEPTH: 58'-6"
FOUNDATION: SLAB

SEARCH ONLINE @ EPLANS.COM

The tiled roof, open gables, and balcony railing give this home traditional Spanish styling that would spice up any neighborhood. Inside, a gallery hall leads both the formal and casual living areas: the living/dining room features a box-bay window and access to a covered patio, and the family room includes a fireplace and a wall of windows. The efficient kitchen boasts a cooktop island with a seating area. Upstairs, a flex room with a wet bar joins the master suite and two secondary bedrooms.

SANTA FE & PUEBLO-STYLE HOMES

Typical Pueblo and Santa Fe influences—thick walls, a flat roof and projecting vigas define this Southwestern home.
Plan HPT810063; see page 115 for details.

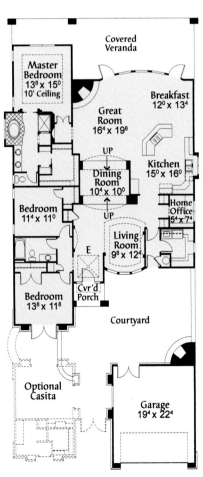

Covered
Veranda

**Master
Bedroom**
13⁸ x 15⁰
10' Ceiling

Breakfast
12⁰ x 13⁴

**Great
Room**
16⁴ x 19⁸

UP

**Dining
Room**
10⁴ x 10⁰

Kitchen
15⁰ x 16⁰

Bedroom
11⁴ x 11⁰

UP

**Home
Office**
5⁴ x 7⁴

**Living
Room**
9⁸ x 12⁴

E

Bedroom
13⁸ x 11⁸

**Cvr'd
Porch**

Courtyard

**Optional
Casita**

Garage
19⁴ x 22⁴

plan⊕ HPT810033

STYLE: PUEBLO
SQUARE FOOTAGE: 2,256
BEDROOMS: 3
BATHROOMS: 2
WIDTH: 46'-4"
DEPTH: 103'-4"
FOUNDATION: SLAB

SEARCH ONLINE @ EPLANS.COM

This modern take on Southwestern style combines an intriguing floor plan and abundant natural light for a home that is a joy to own. From the skylit entry, the bayed living room resides to the right. Just ahead, the dining room is raised up a step, lending a dramatic sense of elegance. Continue past the petite home office to the open kitchen, where a cooktop island overlooks the great room's corner hearth. A bowed window at the rear ushers in cheerful sunlight. The master suite is designed to pamper, with French doors and a tiled garden tub.

plan# HPT810034

STYLE: PUEBLO
SQUARE FOOTAGE: 2,734
BEDROOMS: 4
BATHROOMS: 3
WIDTH: 63'-4"
DEPTH: 92'-4"
FOUNDATION: SLAB

SEARCH ONLINE @ EPLANS.COM

Sun country gets a fresh face on this contemporary Southwestern home. A side-loading garage makes this design great for a corner lot; inside, the floor plan caters to a family who loves to entertain. Enter to find the living room to the right; a fireplace lends a focal point to the space. The dining room is raised up a step for dramatic elegance, creating a unique traffic flow. The hearth-warmed family room boasts four doors to the rear veranda and opens to a gourmet island kitchen. Although every bedroom enjoys patio access, it is the master suite that really shines. Here, a private patio with a fireplace (which shares its warmth with the veranda) is great in any weather. The compartmented bath highlights a whirlpool tub and generous walk-in closet.

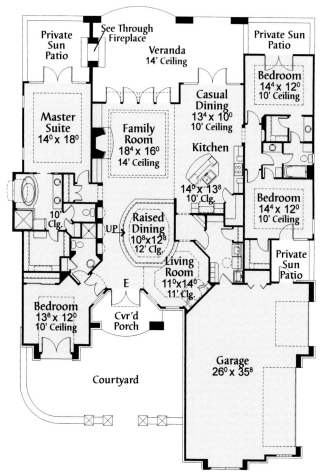

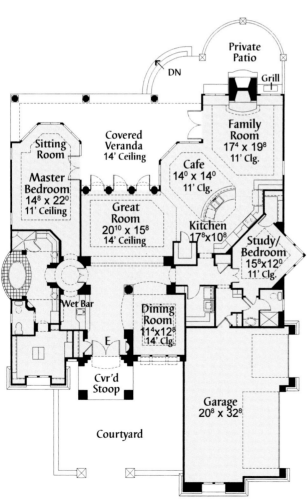

A large courtyard and an elegant double-door entry provide a wonderful introduction to this Pueblo-style design. Inside, a triple window brings natural light to the dining room, and a wet bar sits just beyond the entry. The central great room, with a soaring 14-foot ceiling, features three doors that open to the covered rear veranda. The kitchen boasts a walk-in pantry and shares a snack bar with a casual "cafe" area. The nearby family room shares a through-fireplace with the veranda. Sleeping quarters include a stunning master suite with a private sitting area and one secondary bedroom that doubles as a study. Both bedrooms feature walk-in closets.

plan# HPT810036

STYLE: PUEBLO
SQUARE FOOTAGE: 1,950
BEDROOMS: 3
BATHROOMS: 2
WIDTH: 65'-4"
DEPTH: 60'-0"
FOUNDATION: SLAB

SEARCH ONLINE @ EPLANS.COM

Clean lines and plenty of windows add style to this contemporary Pueblo design. A fireplace makes the expansive entry courtyard even more welcoming. Inside, another fireplace, a wet bar and a curved wall of windows enhance the great room. The kitchen easily serves the formal dining room and the breakfast area, which opens to a covered rear veranda. A split-bedroom plan places the master suite, with its indulgent dual-vanity bath and walk-in closet, to the right of the plan; two family bedrooms sit to the left of the plan.

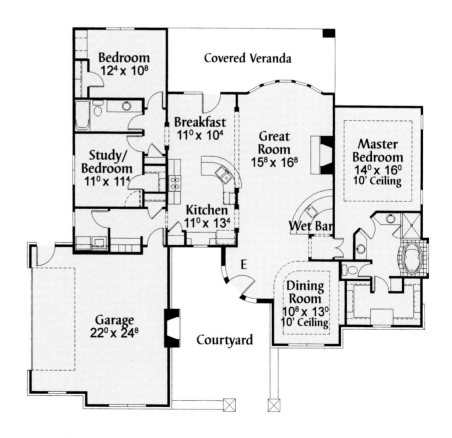

LOWER LEVEL

BEDRM 13⁸ x 12⁸

BEDRM 10⁰ x 19⁰

COVERED PATIO

GREAT RM 20² x 18⁰

STORAGE

BATH

MAIN LEVEL

MASTER BEDRM 18⁰ x 14⁰

COVERED DECK

MASTER BATH

WALK-IN CLOSET

BATH

LIVING RM 20² x 19⁰

BEDRM 12⁰ x 12⁶

LAUNDRY

FOYER

DINING 13⁴ x 11⁸

RAILING

COVERED PORCH

PANTRY

GARAGE 20⁰ x 29¹⁰

KIT 10⁰ x 9⁰

BRKFST 8⁸ x 8⁸

plan# HPT810037

STYLE: PUEBLO
MAIN LEVEL: 1,946 SQ. FT.
LOWER LEVEL: 956 SQ. FT.
TOTAL: 2,902 SQ. FT.
BEDROOMS: 4
BATHROOMS: 3
WIDTH: 51'-6"
DEPTH: 70'-2"
FOUNDATION: BASEMENT

SEARCH ONLINE @ EPLANS.COM

The simple, Pueblo-style lines borrowed from ear[?] Native American dwellings combine with contempora[?] planning for the best possible design. From the front, th[?] home appears to be a one-story. However, a lower level pr[?] vides a two-story rear elevation, making it ideal for slopi[?] lots. The unique floor plan places a circular staircase to th[?] left of the angled foyer. To the right is an L-shaped kitche[?] with a walk-in pantry, a sun-filled breakfast room and[?] formal dining room. Half-walls border the entrance to th[?] formal living room that is warmed by a beehive fireplac[?] The adjacent covered deck provides shade to the pat[?] below. A roomy master suite, secondary bedroom, full ba[?] and laundry room complete the first floor. The lower lev[?] contains a great room, a full bath and two family bedroom[?]

plan# HPT810038

STYLE: PUEBLO
SQUARE FOOTAGE: 1,841
BEDROOMS: 3
BATHROOMS: 2
WIDTH: 55'-8"
DEPTH: 78'-0"
FOUNDATION: SLAB

SEARCH ONLINE @ EPLANS.COM

Three fireplaces—one in the courtyard, a second in the great room, and a third on the private master-suite patio—add extra warmth to this new Pueblo-style home. This design also boasts a great indoor/outdoor relationship: the dining room opens to the courtyard, and the great room and breakfast area both feature French doors that open to a covered rear veranda. Other notable features include built-in shelves in the great room, a spa tub in the master bath and a built-in grill on the veranda.

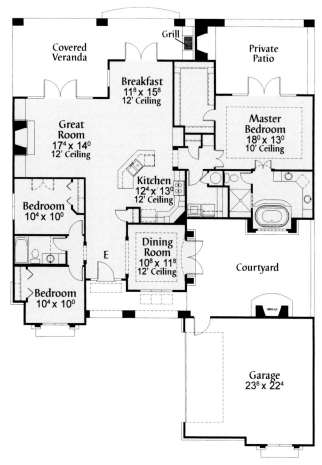

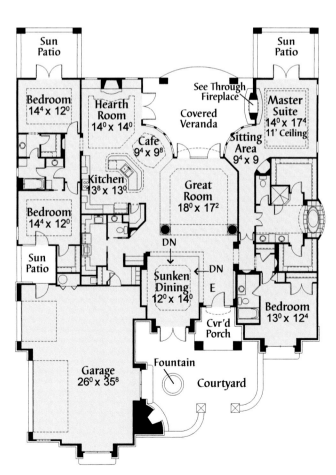

plan# HPT810039

STYLE: SANTA FE
SQUARE FOOTAGE: 3,231
BEDROOMS: 4
BATHROOMS: 3½
WIDTH: 72'-2"
DEPTH: 96'-8"
FOUNDATION: SLAB

SEARCH ONLINE @ EPLANS.COM

Ambitious angles and captivating details give distinctive personality to this Southwest-inspired home. Inside, dramatic features include a sunken dining room, prominent great-room columns, and symmetrical rear bowed windows. Natural light floods the efficient island kitchen and adjacent "cafe." The cozy hearth room opens to the covered veranda, complemented by a see-through fireplace shared with the master bedroom. A private sitting room and magnificent bath are a glorious addition to the master suite. Each of the four bedrooms has private patio access.

plan # HPT810040

STYLE: SANTA FE
FIRST FLOOR: 1,716 SQ. FT.
SECOND FLOOR: 1,543 SQ. FT.
TOTAL: 3,259 SQ. FT.
BEDROOMS: 4
BATHROOMS: 3½
WIDTH: 63'-4"
DEPTH: 69'-0"
FOUNDATION: SLAB

SEARCH ONLINE @ EPLANS.COM

Authentic Southwestern appeal begins with the rustic covered porch, and Pueblo-style roof on this lively home. The well-lit entry opens on the left to a formal dining room with French doors to the wrapping porch. The bon vivant kitchen allows for a compact home office and walk-in pantry. Just ahead, the casual family dining area opens to the rear veranda, where a fireplace and grill await year-round fun. An impressive great room is warmed by a second fireplace. Yet another cozy fireplace lends romance to the gracious master suite, revered for its private patio and resplendent spa bath. Upstairs, each bedroom—plus the upper-level family room—has patio access. A computer niche is great for students.

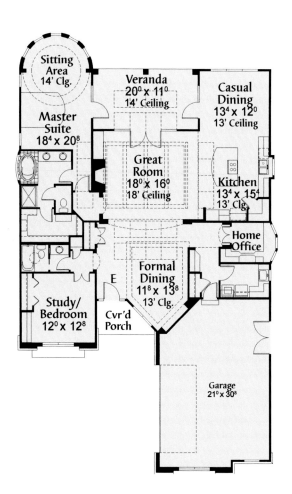

plan# HPT810041

STYLE: SANTA FE
SQUARE FOOTAGE: 2,058
BEDROOMS: 2
BATHROOMS: 2
WIDTH: 49'-11"
DEPTH: 82'-0"
FOUNDATION: SLAB

SEARCH ONLINE @ EPLANS.COM

This contemporary Southwestern home is designed with modern amenities and style that will please your family for years to come. Inside, the skylit entry opens on the right to a formal dining room, defined by a tray ceiling. The great room is graced by an eighteen-foot ceiling and a cozy fireplace. The cooktop island kitchen views the fireplace and casual dining area. A bayed home office is great for telecommuters and students. In the master suite, a semi-circular sitting area is bathed in light. A private bath with a whirlpool tub is a thoughtful addition. Another bedroom at the front of the plan makes a fine study. Not to be missed: a rear skylit veranda for outdoor relaxation.

plan# HPT810042

STYLE: SANTA FE
FIRST FLOOR: 1,527 SQ. FT.
SECOND FLOOR: 1,611 SQ. FT.
TOTAL: 3,138 SQ. FT.
BEDROOMS: 5
BATHROOMS: 4½
WIDTH: 54'-0"
DEPTH: 67'-0"
FOUNDATION: SLAB

SEARCH ONLINE @ EPLANS.COM

This villa-style Southwestern home invokes the use of arches and slightly pitched roofs to balance a squared-off stucco facade. Enter the main level to a living room/dining room on the left. Ahead, an open island kitchen views the gathering room's focal fireplace. The sunny breakfast nook opens on either end to a rear veranda. A guest suite near the kitchen offers a private courtyard. Upstairs, outdoor spaces include a veranda, master patio and hearth-warmed patio. The master suite is a decadent retreat with a vaulted spa bath and huge walk-in closet. Two more bedrooms access the upper-level family room, or turn into a splendid bedroom.

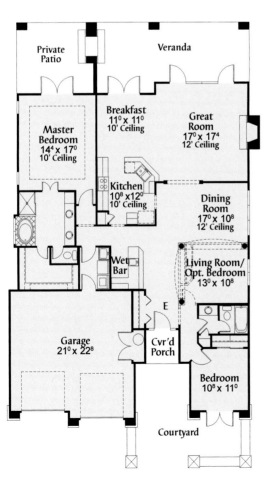

plan⊕ HPT810043

STYLE: SW CONTEMPORARY
SQUARE FOOTAGE: 1,899
BEDROOMS: 3
BATHROOMS: 2
WIDTH: 43'-4"
DEPTH: 79'-6"
FOUNDATION: SLAB

SEARCH ONLINE @ EPLANS.COM

Long and slender, this Pueblo-style home is perfec
for a narrow lot. A facade graced with stepped roofline
and vigas brings the Southwest to your neighborhoo
The well-lit entry begins with a columned living room–
enclose the space for a generous bedroom. Ahead, th
wet bar and dining room are ready to serve guests i
style. Continue through arches to the hearth-warme
great room and breakfast nook, both with verand
access. The secluded master suite is located to the fa
left, splendid with an indulgent bath and private patio.

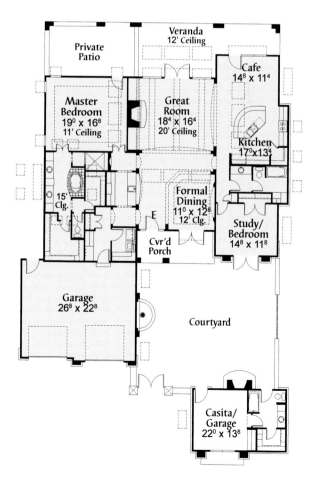

plan# HPT810044

STYLE: PUEBLO
SQUARE FOOTAGE: 2,331
BEDROOMS: 3
BATHROOMS: 3
WIDTH: 63'-8"
DEPTH: 100'-4"
FOUNDATION: SLAB

SEARCH ONLINE @ EPLANS.COM

A contemporary spin on Western style, this well-planned pueblo is full of the amenities you want—and a few extras you'll love! Enter from a single glass door to the foyer, or through double glass doors to the formal dining room. A quiet study, or make it a bedroom, also opens to the front courtyard. In the great room, a soaring twenty-foot ceiling is balanced by an extended-hearth fireplace and floods of natural light, afforded by rear French doors. Relax in lavish comfort in the master suite, complete with a box-vault ceiling, skylights and a pampering whirlpool bath. Not to be missed: a private casita with a full bath and an outdoor fireplace.

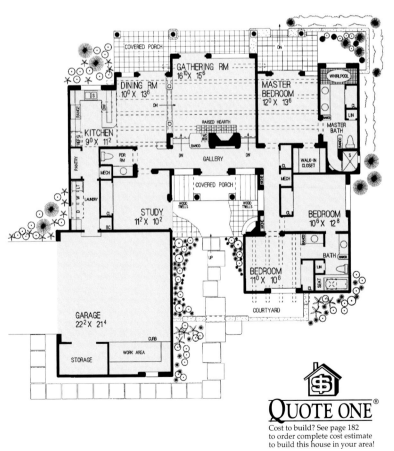

plan# HPT810045

STYLE: SANTA FE
SQUARE FOOTAGE: 1,907
BEDROOMS: 3
BATHROOMS: 2½
WIDTH: 61'-6"
DEPTH: 67'-4"
FOUNDATION: SLAB

SEARCH ONLINE @ EPLANS.COM

Graceful curves welcome you into the courtyard of this Santa Fe home. Inside, a gallery directs traffic to the work zone on the left or the sleeping zone on the right. The wide covered rear porch is accessible from the dining room, gathering room (with a fireplace) and secluded master bedroom. The master bath features a whirlpool tub, separate shower, double vanity and a spacious walk-in closet. Two additional bedrooms share a full bath with separate vanities. Extra storage space is provided in the two-car garage.

QUOTE ONE®

Cost to build? See page 182
to order complete cost estimate
to build this house in your area!

plan# HPT810046

STYLE: SANTA FE
SQUARE FOOTAGE: 2,945
BEDROOMS: 4
BATHROOMS: 2½
WIDTH: 73'-0"
DEPTH: 68'-10"
FOUNDATION: SLAB

SEARCH ONLINE @ EPLANS.COM

Flat roofs, soft, curved wall lines, masses of stucco, exposed rafter tails, an arched privacy wall, carriage lamps and a courtyard are the distinguishing factors of this Pueblo-style ranch house. Inside, twin archways provide access to the beam-ceilinged family room. The modified U-shaped kitchen and its breakfast area are open to the family room. The kitchen will be a delight in which to work with its island, pantry and fine counter space. Down the hall are four bedrooms and two baths. Each of three secondary bedrooms is sizable and handy to the bath with double lavatories. The master suite is outstanding, with direct patio access.

Quote One®
Cost to build? See page 182
to order complete cost estimate
to build this house in your area!

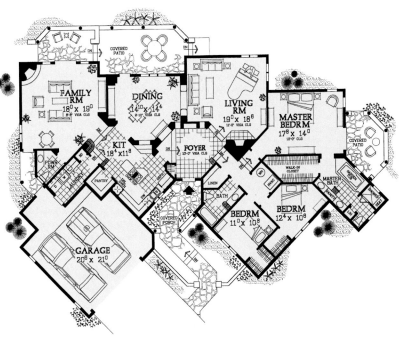

plan# HPT810047

STYLE: SANTA FE
SQUARE FOOTAGE: 2,582
BEDROOMS: 3
BATHROOMS: 2½
WIDTH: 87'-4"
DEPTH: 65'-10"
FOUNDATION: SLAB

SEARCH ONLINE @ EPLANS.COM

This home is made to order for a slightl
sloping lot—or have your site graded to fit its con
tours! The classic Pueblo styling includes projectin
vigas, rounded corners and rough-sawn lintels. Ente
by way of a walled courtyard that protects the entry
The central foyer gives way to a large living roor
(there's space for a baby grand!) and the bedrooms o
the right. The master suite opens to a private covere
patio and has a bath with a gigantic walk-in closet,
garden tub and a separate shower. The formal dinin
room features a covered patio for alfresco meals an
connects to the island kitchen for easy entertainin;
For casual occasions, the family room serves up
corner fireplace and access to yet another patio are
The two-car garage includes plenty of storage space

plan# HPT810048

STYLE: SANTA FE
SQUARE FOOTAGE: 2,276
BEDROOMS: 4
BATHROOMS: 2½
WIDTH: 61'-6"
DEPTH: 73'-4"
FOUNDATION: SLAB

SEARCH ONLINE @ EPLANS.COM

The great room, dining room and master bedroom all open to the covered patio that extends the width of this Southwestern home, offering plenty of space for relaxing and entertaining. The dining room is open to the kitchen with its window sink, large pantry and adjacent laundry room. From this side of the plan, a gallery leads from the powder room and study to the bedroom wing, where two secondary bedrooms share a connecting bath that has separate vanities. Opposite these bedrooms, the master suite includes a walk-in closet and a compartmented bath with a whirlpool tub.

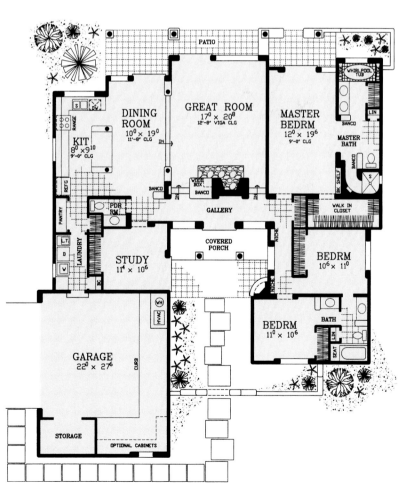

An in-line floor plan follows the tradition of the original Santa Fe-style homes. The slight curve to the overall configuration lends an interesting touch. From the front courtyard, the plan opens to a formal living room and dining room, complemented by a family room and a kitchen with an adjoining morning room. The master suite is found to one side of the plan while family bedrooms share space at the opposite end. There's also a huge office and a bonus/study area for private times.

QUOTE ONE®

Cost to build? See page 182
to order complete cost estimate
to build this house in your area!

plan# HPT810049

L

STYLE: SANTA FE
SQUARE FOOTAGE: 3,428
BEDROOMS: 4
BATHROOMS: 3½
WIDTH: 120'-0"
DEPTH: 86'-0"
FOUNDATION: SLAB

SEARCH ONLINE @ EPLANS.COM

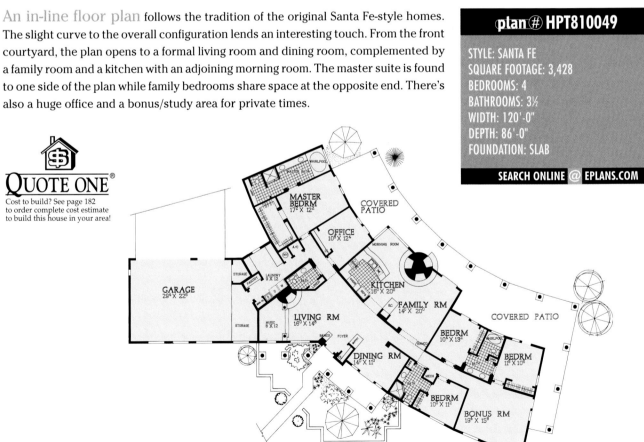

plan# HPT810050

STYLE: SANTA FE
SQUARE FOOTAGE: 2,015
BEDROOMS: 3
BATHROOMS: 2½
WIDTH: 96'-5"
DEPTH: 54'-9"
FOUNDATION: SLAB

SEARCH ONLINE @ EPLANS.COM

QUOTE ONE®

Cost to build? See page 182
to order complete cost estimate
to build this house in your area!

This Santa Fe-style home is as warm as a desert breeze and just as comfortable. Outside details are reminiscent of old-style adobe homes, while the interior caters to convenient living. The front covered porch leads to an open foyer. Columns define the formal dining room and the giant great room. The kitchen has an enormous pantry and a snack bar and is connected to a breakfast nook with rear-patio access. Two family bedrooms on the right side of the plan share a full bathroom that includes twin vanities. The master suite on the left side of the plan has a monstrous walk-in closet and a bath with a spa-style tub and a separate shower.

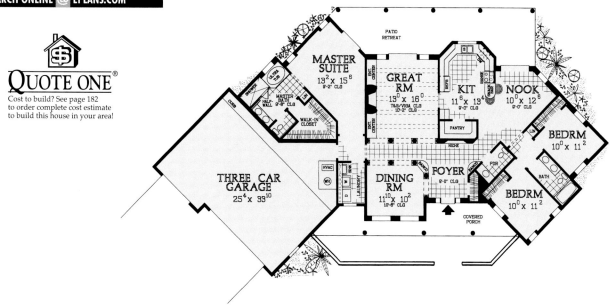

The two-level rear patio of this design brings a new dimension to outdoor living. Patio access is from the foyer, family room and great room. The family room features a corner fireplace with a raised hearth, and a snack bar off the U-shaped kitchen, which has an island cooktop and a walk-in pantry. A second fireplace, also with a raised hearth, warms the great room. The master suite opens to a private courtyard and includes a compartmented bath with separate shower and garden tub, a double-bowl vanity and a walk-in closet. Two family bedrooms at the front of the plan offer walk-in closets and share a bath.

plan⊕ HPT810051

STYLE: SANTA FE
SQUARE FOOTAGE: 2,741
BEDROOMS: 3
BATHROOMS: 2½
WIDTH: 98'-0"
DEPTH: 59'-0"
FOUNDATION: SLAB

SEARCH ONLINE @ EPLANS.COM

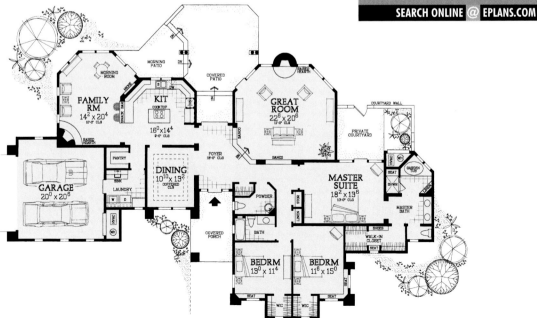

plan# HPT810052

L

STYLE: SANTA FE
SQUARE FOOTAGE: 2,092
BEDROOMS: 3
BATHROOMS: 2½
WIDTH: 85'-9"
DEPTH: 67'-10"
FOUNDATION: SLAB

SEARCH ONLINE @ EPLANS.COM

Stucco exterior walls highlighted by simple window treatments and effective glass-block patterns introduce a fine, Western-style home. High ceilings and open planning contribute to the spaciousness of the interior. The large foyer effectively routes traffic to the main living areas. To the left is the angular formal dining room with its half walls and tray ceiling. Straight ahead from the double front doors is the formal living room, which features a beamed ceiling and a commanding corner fireplace with a raised hearth and bench. French doors open to the covered rear patio. Past the built-in bookshelves of the family room is the hallway to the sleeping zone, which consists of a master suite and two secondary bedrooms.

QUOTE ONE®
Cost to build? See page 182
to order complete cost estimate
to build this house in your area!

The impressive, double-door entry to the walled courtyard sets the tone for this Santa Fe masterpiece home. The expansive great room shows off its casual style with a centerpiece fireplace and abundant windows overlooking the patio. Joining the great room is the formal dining room, graced with windows and patio doors. The large gourmet kitchen has an eat-in snack bar and joins the family room to create a warm atmosphere for casual entertaining. Family-room extras include a fireplace, entertainment built-ins and double doors to the front courtyard. Just off the family room are the two large family bedrooms, which share a private bath. The relaxing master suite is located off the great room and has double doors to the back patio.

plan# HPT810053

L

STYLE: SANTA FE
SQUARE FOOTAGE: 2,226
BEDROOMS: 3
BATHROOMS: 2½
WIDTH: 103'-1"
DEPTH: 71'-11"
FOUNDATION: SLAB

SEARCH ONLINE @ EPLANS.COM

QUOTE ONE®
Cost to build? See page 182
to order complete cost estimate
to build this house in your area!

plan# HPT810054

STYLE: SANTA FE
SQUARE FOOTAGE: 2,922
BEDROOMS: 2
BATHROOMS: 2½
WIDTH: 82'-0"
DEPTH: 77'-0"
FOUNDATION: SLAB

SEARCH ONLINE @ EPLANS.COM

This one-story home matches traditional southwestern design elements such as stucco, tile and exposed rafters (vigas) with an up-to-date floor plan. The vast gathering room provides a dramatic multi-purpose living area. Interesting angles highlight the kitchen, which offers plenty of counter and cabinet space, a planning desk, a snack-bar pass-through into the gathering room, and a morning room with a bumped-out bay. A media room could serve as a third bedroom. The luxurious master bedroom contains a walk-in closet and an amenity-filled bath with a whirlpool tub. A three-car garage easily serves the family fleet.

QUOTE ONE®
Cost to build? See page 182
to order complete cost estimate
to build this house in your area!

This diamond in the desert gives new meaning to old style. A courtyard leads to a covered porch with nooks for sitting and open-air dining. The gracious living room is highlighted by a corner fireplace, while the formal dining room comes with an adjacent butler's pantry and access to the porch dining area. Two sleeping zones are luxurious with whirlpool tubs and separate showers. The master suite also boasts an exercise room and a nearby private office. A guest suite includes a private entrance and another corner fireplace.

plan# HPT810055

STYLE: SANTA FE
SQUARE FOOTAGE: 3,838
BEDROOMS: 4
BATHROOMS: 3½
WIDTH: 127'-6"
DEPTH: 60'-10"
FOUNDATION: SLAB

SEARCH ONLINE @ EPLANS.COM

QUOTE ONE®
Cost to build? See page 182
to order complete cost estimate
to build this house in your area!

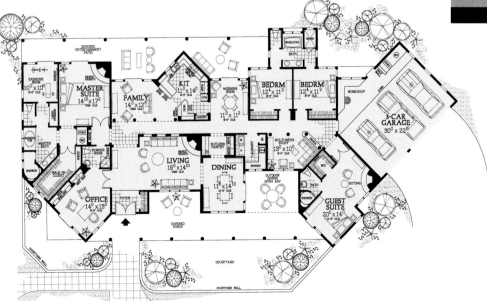

TO ORDER BLUEPRINTS CALL TOLL FREE 1-800-521-67

plan# HPT810056

L

STYLE: SANTA FE
SQUARE FOOTAGE: 3,169
BEDROOMS: 4
BATHROOMS: 3½
WIDTH: 120'-0"
DEPTH: 76'-0"
FOUNDATION: SLAB

SEARCH ONLINE @ EPLANS.COM

QUOTE ONE®
Cost to build? See page 182
to order complete cost estimate
to build this house in your area!

Projecting wood beams, or vigas, add a distinctive touch to this Santa Fe exterior. A private courtyard leads to the entryway of this radially planned home. To the left of the foyer rests a living room with a wood-beamed ceiling, music alcove and fireplace. Past the formal dining room on the right are the family room and large country kitchen with snack bar and morning room. The focal point of this casual living zone is the massive fireplace. Three family bedrooms, two full baths and an open study with adjoining courtyard round out the right wing. Wood-beams and an oversized, spa-style bath give the master suite a posh attitude. Completing this wing is an office, powder room, laundry/utility room and a three-car garage with work room.

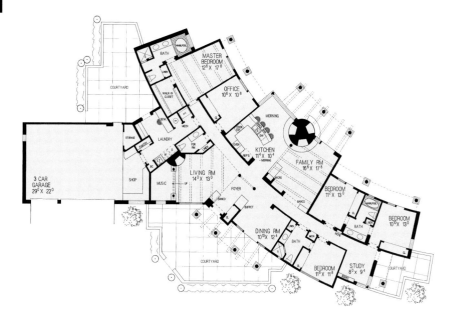

Angled living spaces add interest to this already magnificent Santa Fe home. From the offset entry you can travel straight back to the open gathering room—or turn to the right to enter the formal living and dining rooms. The huge kitchen is centralized and features an L-shaped work area with an island. Secondary bedrooms open to a side patio and share a full bath. The master suite is complemented by a warm study and is separated from the secondary bedrooms for privacy.

plan# HPT810057

L

STYLE: SANTA FE
SQUARE FOOTAGE: 2,624
BEDROOMS: 4
BATHROOMS: 3
WIDTH: 88'-8"
DEPTH: 69'-0"
FOUNDATION: SLAB

SEARCH ONLINE @ EPLANS.COM

QUOTE ONE®

Cost to build? See page 182 to order complete cost estimate to build this house in your area!

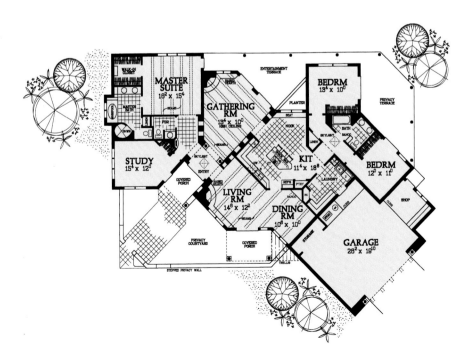

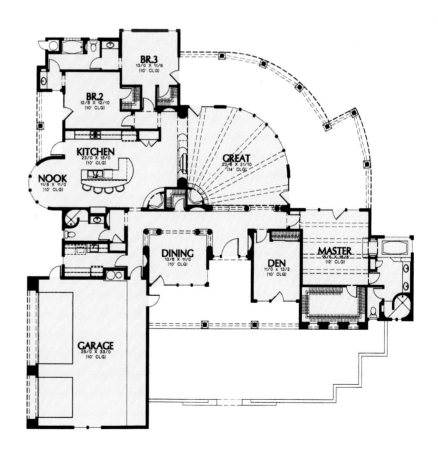

plan# HPT810125

STYLE: SANTA FE
SQUARE FOOTAGE: 3,260
BEDROOMS: 3
BATHROOMS: 3
WIDTH: 90'-0"
DEPTH: 89'-6"
FOUNDATION: SLAB

SEARCH ONLINE @ EPLANS.COM

Striking good looks and attention to detail make this Santa Fe design a winner in any neighborhood. An arched half-wall entry leads to a courtyard and a slightly recessed entry. Just past the foyer, a "banco" wall provides plant shelves or an entertainment center in the great room. An architectural array of vigas emphasizes the scallop-shaped glass wall, culminating in a beehive fireplace. The kitchen is ready to serve the bow-windowed nook and elegant dining room, with an ample island that seats four, and a cozy hearth. Secondary bedrooms are located nearby. The master suite is situated for privacy and enjoys a viga-topped ceiling, romantic fireplace, and fantastic bath.

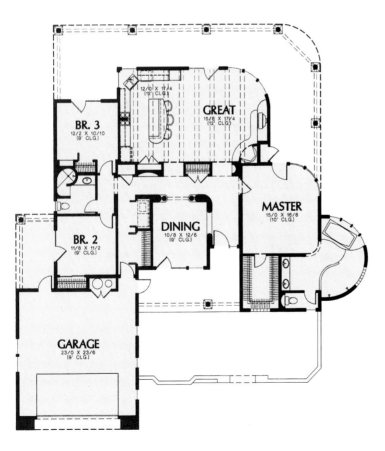

plan# HPT810126

STYLE: PUEBLO
SQUARE FOOTAGE: 2,992
BEDROOMS: 3
BATHROOMS: 2½
WIDTH: 82'-0"
DEPTH: 90'-4"
FOUNDATION: SLAB

SEARCH ONLINE @ EPLANS.COM

This beautiful Pueblo-style home combines the his
toric intrigue of Native American architecture with a floor
plan that is designed for today's active family. Enter past a
stucco arch to find the foyer; columns and front-porch
access lend elegance to the nearby dining room. Art niches
mark the great room, where a beehive fireplace and bowed
window wall make a grand impression. A snack-bar island
in the L-shaped kitchen is perfect for casual meals; the
corner sink is thoughtfully set in bright windows.
Secondary bedrooms reside on the left, each with patio
access. A shared bath includes an inventive curved shower.
In the master suite, natural light pours in from the bowed
window, enhanced by a ten-foot ceiling. The semi-circular
master bath is remarkable, with a garden tub, walk-up
shower (with dual heads) and compartmented toilet.

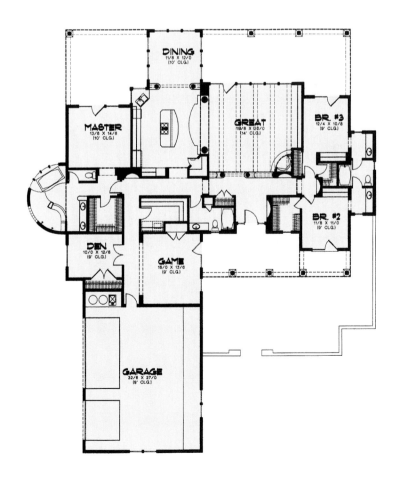

plan# HPT810127

STYLE: PUEBLO
SQUARE FOOTAGE: 3,060
BEDROOMS: 3
BATHROOMS: 3
WIDTH: 82'-0"
DEPTH: 95'-6"
FOUNDATION: SLAB

SEARCH ONLINE @ EPLANS.COM

Stepped roof accents join a Spanish-tile topped porch for a traditional Pueblo home with wonderful amenities inside. Enter to a prominent foyer, adorned with a niche. Just ahead, columns introduce the great room; a focal-point beehive hearth warms as a rear wall of windows brightens the space. The cooktop-island kitchen is designed to work hard, so burgeoning chefs can create gourmet meals with ease. An extended dining area is surrounded by windows for a cheerful presence. Follow a gallery hall to the master suite, where patio access and a bumped-out deluxe bath are simply outstanding. The game room, with porch access, is prepared to entertain young and old alike.

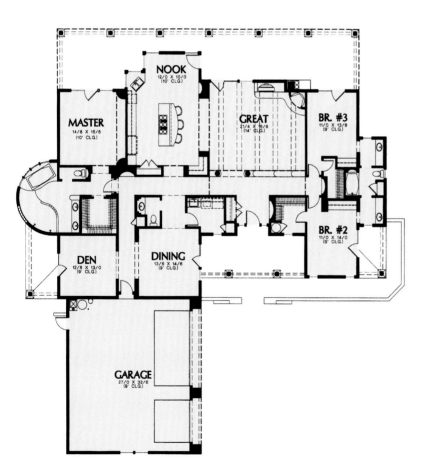

plan# HPT810128

STYLE: SANTA FE
SQUARE FOOTAGE: 2,992
BEDROOMS: 3
BATHROOMS: 2½
WIDTH: 82'-0"
DEPTH: 90'-4"
FOUNDATION: SLAB

SEARCH ONLINE @ EPLANS.COM

Cubic angles, decorative vigas and a ranch style porch provide authentic Southwest flavo to this generous home. A recessed entry open to the foyer and columned great room. Vintag beams top the fourteen-foot ceiling, balanced b a raised beehive fireplace. Follow an arc through thick walls to the gourmet kitche Here, space for a six-burner cooktop on th snack-bar island adds gourmet flavor, as th corner window ushers in light. Tucked to th rear, the master suite enjoys raised ceiling rear patio access, and a spectacular curved bat with a windowed garden tub and walk-in show built for two. Secondary bedrooms share a we designed bath on the right side of the plan. Bo the den and dining room feature outdoor acces

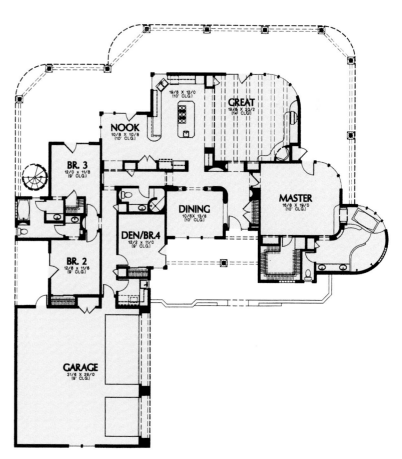

plan# HPT810129

STYLE: PUEBLO
SQUARE FOOTAGE: 2,941
BEDROOMS: 3
BATHROOMS: 3
WIDTH: 97'-0"
DEPTH: 89'-0"
FOUNDATION: SLAB

SEARCH ONLINE @ EPLANS.COM

Whether surrounded by saguaros or sky-scrapers, this Southwestern home will be a joy for years to come. A Mission-style arch greets friends and family, leading to a shaded front porch. Inside, a coat closet and art niche accent the foyer. A thick Pueblo wall, with inset niches, announces the great room; a rustic beam ceiling soars fourteen feet overhead. Designed for striking vistas, the rear window wall affords panoramic views. The glow of the beehive fireplace can be enjoyed from the cooktop-island kitchen, created to serve the elegant dining room and light-filled nook. Two nearby secondary bedrooms share a full bath with private vanities; the den makes an ideal guest room. For ultimate luxury, the master suite presents a curved window, glass-block-lit closet, and a magnificent bath with a whirlpool tub and dual-head shower.

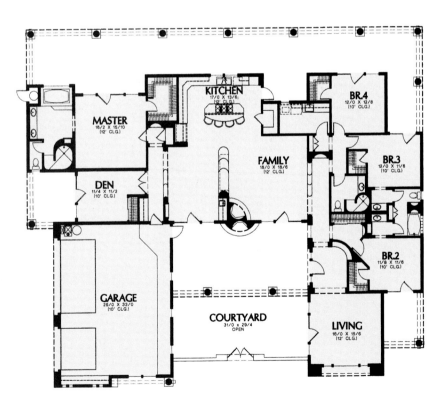

plan# HPT810130

STYLE: PUEBLO
SQUARE FOOTAGE: 3,212
BEDROOMS: 4
BATHROOMS: 3
WIDTH: 90'-0"
DEPTH: 78'-0"
FOUNDATION: SLAB

SEARCH ONLINE @ EPLANS.COM

This grand four-bedroom Pueblo exemplifies Southwestern living at its best. Enter through an arched gate to the courtyard; four main entrances surround an outdoor fireplace. Bring guests in through an impressive side foyer. The living room resides to the right, and a gallery hall leads to the spacious family room. An efficient kitchen features a serving bar with space for a six-burner range and seating for four. Flex space beyond works well as a dining room. A nearby den opens through double doors and accesses a private patio. The adjacent master suite shines with a step-up garden tub, and curved shower. Three secondary bedrooms share two baths on the left side of the home; each bedroom has outdoor access.

plan# HPT810131

STYLE: SANTA FE
SQUARE FOOTAGE: 3,614
BEDROOMS: 3
BATHROOMS: 2½
WIDTH: 96'-0"
DEPTH: 85'-0"
FOUNDATION: SLAB

SEARCH ONLINE @ EPLANS.COM

Come home to a bold Santa Fe design that is made for entertaining! The plan begins with a gated courtyard, surrounded by privacy walls. A fountain and columned loggia join an outdoor fireplace for effortless regaling. Although four rooms access the loggia, the main entrance is to the right, presenting an impressive foyer. A living room greets guests; family bedrooms are located nearby, with patio access. The vast family room is topped with authentic viga beams, and warmed by a beehive hearth. Just ahead, a gourmet kitchen serves at least five hungry family members at the island bar. Casual meals can also be enjoyed in the light-filled nook; the dining room is ready to host with a wet bar and decorative columns. The master suite is a dream come true, complete with a step-up tub, spiral shower and massive walk-in closet.

Here's a rambling ranch with a unique configuration. This well-zoned plan offers exceptional one-story livability for the active family. The central foyer routes traffic effectively while featuring a feeling of spaciousness. Note the dramatic columns that accentuate the big living room with its high ceiling. This interesting, angular room has a commanding corner fireplace with a raised hearth, a wall of windows, a doorway to the huge rear covered porch and a pass-through to the kitchen. The informal family room directly accesses the rear porch and is handy to the three children's bedrooms. At the opposite end of the plan, and guaranteed its full measure of privacy, is the large master suite. The master bedroom, with its high ceiling, enjoys direct access to the rear porch.

plan⊕ HPT810058

L

STYLE: SANTA FE
SQUARE FOOTAGE: 2,966
BEDROOMS: 4
BATHROOMS: 3½
WIDTH: 116'-7"
DEPTH: 77'-5"
FOUNDATION: SLAB

SEARCH ONLINE @ EPLANS.COM

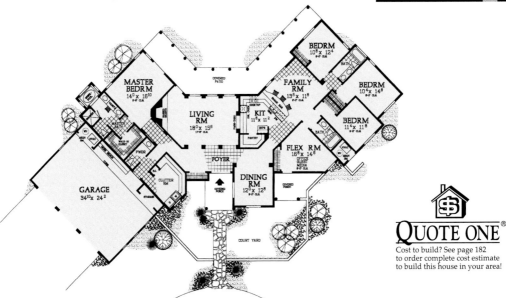

QUOTE ONE®
Cost to build? See page 182
to order complete cost estimate
to build this house in your area!

plan# HPT810059

STYLE: SANTA FE
SQUARE FOOTAGE: 3,959
BEDROOMS: 3
BATHROOMS: 3½
WIDTH: 107'-2"
DEPTH: 81'-3"
FOUNDATION: SLAB

SEARCH ONLINE @ EPLANS.COM

This sensational Santa Fe is more than just a pretty face—it boasts an unrestrained floor plan with bays and niches, as well as soaring, open space. The central foyer leads to the living areas and opens to a spectacular formal living room, with ample space for a baby grand. The nearby dining room offers service from the gourmet kitchen, which features an island cooktop counter. A bayed morning nook accommodates casual meals and leads to the family room, with an extended-hearth fireplace and access to a private covered porch. The rambling master suite is a relaxing retreat for the homeowner, and includes a skylit dressing area, an expansive walk-in closet, an exercise bay with windows and a lavish bath with a windowed tub. Two family bedrooms, each with its own bath, enjoy a secluded wing to the rear of the plan.

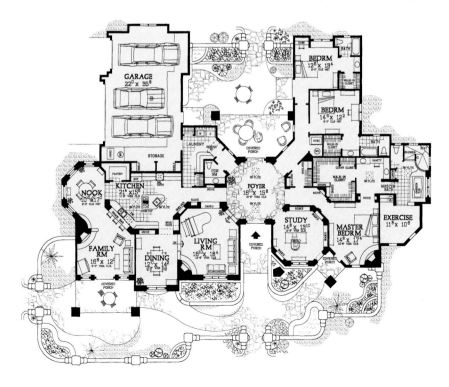

Tame the Wild West with this handsome adobe-style home. Suitable for side-sloping lots, it contains a wealth of livability. An abundance of windows and a raised stucco hearth with a long window-seat bench, or banco, graces the living room. The formal dining room is nearby, creating a lovely space for entertaining. All will enjoy the family room with an adjacent gourmet kitchen and breakfast nook. Split styling puts the master bedroom suite on the right side of the plan. Here, a walk-in closet, whirlpool tub, and curved shower bring a touch of luxury. A private den/sitting room is located within the master bedroom suite. Three upstairs bedrooms share two hall baths.

plan# HPT810060

L

STYLE: SANTA FE
FIRST FLOOR: 2,024 SQ. FT.
SECOND FLOOR: 800 SQ. FT.
TOTAL: 2,824 SQ. FT.
BEDROOMS: 3
BATHROOMS: 3½
WIDTH: 80'-10"
DEPTH: 54'-0"
FOUNDATION: SLAB

SEARCH ONLINE @ EPLANS.COM

QUOTE ONE®
Cost to build? See page 182
to order complete cost estimate
to build this house in your area!

FIRST FLOOR

SECOND FLOOR

plan# HPT810061

STYLE: SANTA FE
SQUARE FOOTAGE: 2,982
BEDROOMS: 4
BATHROOMS: 3½
WIDTH: 88'-6"
DEPTH: 104'-0"
FOUNDATION: SLAB

SEARCH ONLINE @ EPLANS.COM

This Southwestern design represents the best of past and present. The exterior recalls the early architecture of the region when it was newly settled, while the interior caters to present-day tastes. The focal point of the sunken living room is the corner fireplace. The gourmet kitchen boasts a cooktop island, skylight, breakfast nook and access to a covered porch. On the opposite side of the plan, two family bedrooms share a bath and a study, with access to a covered porch. The master suite, at the rear of the home, boasts a corner fireplace, two walk-in closets, a luxurious bath, and a door to a private section of the covered porch.

Frontal views are no problem with this Pueblo-style home. A large front courtyard with easy access to the main bath easily accommodates pool parties. The entry opens onto the great room with a twelve-foot ceiling and a beehive fireplace, and continues to the formal dining room through a thick arch and radius wall. An open kitchen, breakfast room and living room are ideal for gatherings and also work well with formal areas for entertaining. The kitchen includes an eleven-foot bar and looks out the rear to the covered patio. The master suite is close to the study right off the great room. Bedrooms 2 and 3 share the main bath, which can also serve the pool. The covered patio spans the entire front of the home, offering a cool shady place to watch desert sunsets.

plan⊕ HPT810062

STYLE: PUEBLO
SQUARE FOOTAGE: 3,018
BEDROOMS: 3
BATHROOMS: 2½
WIDTH: 95'-0"
DEPTH: 79'-0"
FOUNDATION: SLAB

SEARCH ONLINE @ EPLANS.COM

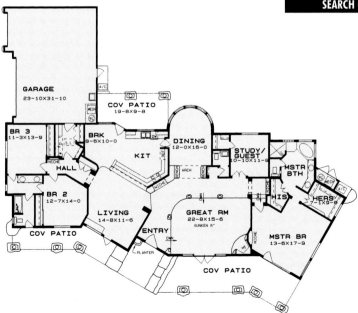

plan# HPT810063

L

STYLE: SANTA FE
FIRST FLOOR: 1,911 SQ. FT.
SECOND FLOOR: 828 SQ. FT.
TOTAL: 2,739 SQ. FT.
BEDROOMS: 4
BATHROOMS: 3½
WIDTH: 87'-10"
DEPTH: 60'-8"
FOUNDATION: SLAB

SEARCH ONLINE @ EPLANS.COM

SECOND FLOOR

FIRST FLOOR

The arched courtyard entrance is a perfect introduction to this plan's wonderful livability—indoors and out. Open spaces and interesting angles greet you at the foyer, which is elegantly intersected with a curved stairway. The formal dining room opens to the large covered patio, perfect for entertaining and outdoor meals. The living room enjoys a dramatic corner fireplace with a raised hearth and is open to the oversized kitchen through a snack bar. A built-in breakfast booth joins the kitchen to the casual family room. The master suite is a welcome retreat thanks to a raised-hearth fireplace, patio door and lavish bath. Up the grand stairway, a lovely window bench frames the hallway leading to two family bedrooms, which share a compartmented bath, and to the guest suite with a private bath.

QUOTE ONE®

Cost to build? See page 182
to order complete cost estimate
to build this house in your area!

SECOND FLOOR

BEDRM 11⁰ x 12⁴
BEDRM 11⁰ x 12⁴
BEDRM 12² x 11⁰
GATHERING ROOM BELOW
BALCONY
BATH
HALLWAY
BALCONY
RAILING
READING LOFT
BOOKSHELVES

plan# HPT810064

STYLE: SANTA FE
FIRST FLOOR: 2,401 SQ. FT.
SECOND FLOOR: 927 SQ. FT.
TOTAL: 3,328 SQ. FT.
BEDROOMS: 4
BATHROOMS: 3
WIDTH: 104'-9"
DEPTH: 62'-5"
FOUNDATION: SLAB

SEARCH ONLINE @ EPLANS.COM

FIRST FLOOR

GARAGE 30² x 22⁴
DINING RM 11⁰ x 11⁰
GATHERING RM 24² x 15¹⁰
MASTER SUITE 15⁰ x 15⁰
BRKFST 11⁰ x 20⁰
STUDY 14⁰ x 12⁴
MEDIA RM 19⁰ x 12⁰
WALK-IN CLOSET
MASTER BATH
LAUNDRY ROOM
GALLERY
FOYER
COVERED PATIO
COVERED PORCH
COVERED PORCH

Honored traditions are echoed throughout th warm and inviting Santa Fe home. A large, two-sto gathering room with a beehive fireplace provides soothing atmosphere for entertaining or quiet inte ludes. A gallery leads to the kitchen and breakfast are where abundant counter space and a work island w please the fussiest of cooks. A nearby laundry roo provides entry to the three-car garage. On the rig side of the plan, the master suite offers a private stud a fireplace and a luxurious bath with dual lavatories whirlpool tub and a curved shower. On the secor floor, a reading loft with built-in bookshelves comp ments three family bedrooms.

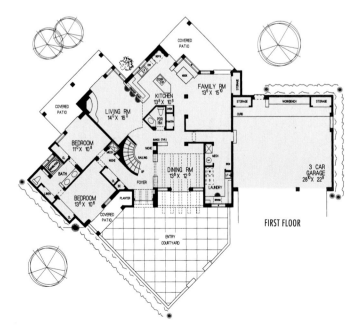

plan# HPT810065 L

STYLE: SANTA FE
FIRST FLOOR: 1,966 SQ. FT.
SECOND FLOOR: 831 SQ. FT.
TOTAL: 2,797 SQ. FT.
BEDROOMS: 4
BATHROOMS: 3½
WIDTH: 90'-0"
DEPTH: 51'-8"
FOUNDATION: SLAB

SEARCH ONLINE @ EPLANS.COM

Unique in nature, this two-story Santa Fe-style home is as practical as it is lovely. The entry foyer leads past a curving staircase to living areas at the back of the plan. These include a living room with a corner fireplace and a family room connected to the kitchen via a built-in eating nook. The kitchen furthers its appeal with an island cooktop and a snack bar. Two family bedrooms on this level include one with a private covered patio. They share a full bath that includes dual lavatories and a whirlpool tub. Upstairs, the master suite features a grand bath, corner fireplace, large walk-in closet and private balcony. A guest bedroom accesses a full bath. Every room in this home has its own outdoor area.

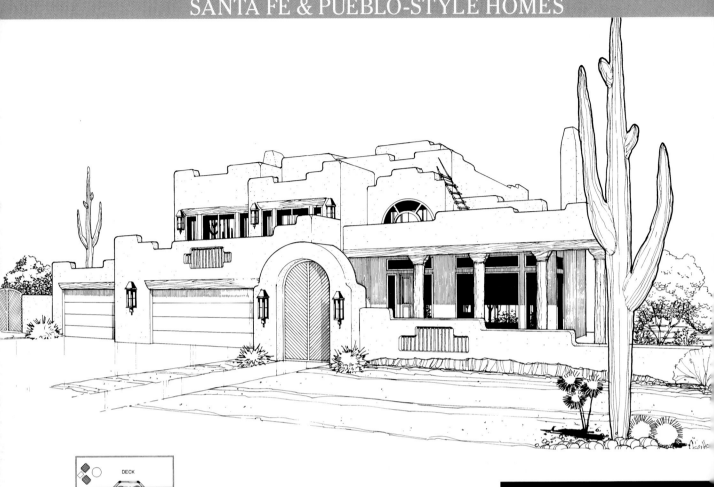

SECOND FLOOR

OPTIONAL SECOND FLOOR

FIRST FLOOR

plan# HPT810066

STYLE: SANTA FE
FIRST FLOOR: 1,166 SQ. FT.
SECOND FLOOR: 995 SQ. FT.
TOTAL: 2,161 SQ. FT.
BEDROOMS: 4
BATHROOMS: 2½
WIDTH: 60'-0"
DEPTH: 53'-6"
FOUNDATION: BASEMENT, SLAB

SEARCH ONLINE @ EPLANS.COM

A blend of Territorial and Pueblo elements makes this a true Southwestern-style home. Formal dining and living rooms have eleven-foot ceilings with log vigas and access to the covered patio. The rear family room is open to the kitchen and a breakfast bay that includes a glass door to the large covered patio. This plan comes with either a three-bedroom or four-bedroom option! The master suite features a double-door entry, log viga ceiling beams and a glass bay with door to a private view deck for lounging. The three-car garage offers extra storage space or room for a boat.

SPANISH COLONIAL & MISSION-STYLE HOMES

Exterior staircases and a multilevel roofline lend Spanish Eclectic style to this design, which also incorporates the ornate windows of Mission-style architecture. Plan HPT810073; see 126 for details.

Warm Spanish stucco creates an inviting appeal on this delightful Southwestern home. The foyer presents an archway to the dining room and family room. A modified galley kitchen gives the impression of an island workspace, and flows into the casual eating area. The master bedroom is graced with a tray ceiling, two closets—one a generous walk-in—and a relaxing bath with a spa tub. Two family bedrooms are thoughtfully placed at the front of the plan. A two-car garage includes a service entrance through the utility room.

plan# HPT810067

STYLE: SPANISH COLONIAL
SQUARE FOOTAGE: 1,782
BEDROOMS: 3
BATHROOMS: 2
WIDTH: 59'-4"
DEPTH: 41'-8"
FOUNDATION: SLAB

SEARCH ONLINE @ EPLANS.COM

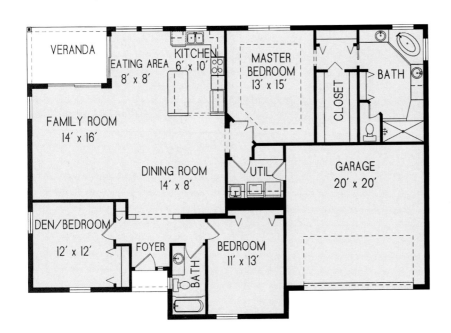

TO ORDER BLUEPRINTS CALL TOLL FREE 1-800-521-679

plan# HPT810068

STYLE: SPANISH COLONIAL
SQUARE FOOTAGE: 2,050
BEDROOMS: 3
BATHROOMS: 2½
WIDTH: 58'-0"
DEPTH: 70'-0"
FOUNDATION: SLAB

SEARCH ONLINE @ EPLANS.COM

Striking exterior details celebrate historic architecture in this lovely Spanish Colonial home. From the rustic front porch, the foyer opens to dining room, defined by a decorative column, and a living room with expansive views of the rear property. To the left, the gourmet kitchen is equipped with counter space galore and easy access to the breakfast nook. A cozy gathering room is flooded with natural light, and opens to the pool area. Two secondary bedrooms complete this wing. The master suite is secluded to the far right, enjoying an enormous walk-in closet, an indulgent bath, and as an added extra, a private cabana bath accessing the lanai.

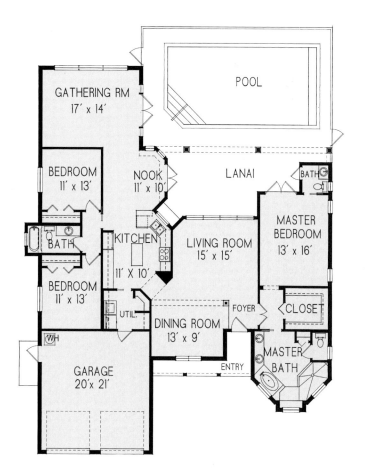

plan# HPT810069

STYLE: SPANISH COLONIAL
SQUARE FOOTAGE: 2,226
BEDROOMS: 3
BATHROOMS: 2½
WIDTH: 59'-5"
DEPTH: 85'-6"
FOUNDATION: SLAB

SEARCH ONLINE @ EPLANS.COM

Welcome home to the simple elegance of Spanish Colonial style. A gate
entry leads to the foyer, which opens to
the great room. A cozy fireplace with surrounding built-ins can be viewed from the
kitchen, decked out with an island and
walk-in pantry. The formal dining room
may also be used as a study; French
doors to the covered porch make this
room great for any occasion. Separated
for privacy, the master suite relishes a
box-bay sitting area, splendid bath and
oversized walk-in closet. Two additional
bedrooms share a full bath.

plan⊞ HPT810070

STYLE: SPANISH COLONIAL
FIRST FLOOR: 2,810 SQ. FT.
SECOND FLOOR: 750 SQ. FT.
TOTAL: 3,560 SQ. FT.
BEDROOMS: 3
BATHROOMS: 3½
WIDTH: 60'-0"
DEPTH: 145'-0"
FOUNDATION: SLAB

SEARCH ONLINE @ EPLANS.COM

Enjoy the warmth and beauty of Spanish Colonial design in this luxurious family home. Designed with privacy in mind, a loggia splits the art room (thoughtfully providing a full bath) from the beamed-ceiling living areas. The family room and breakfast nook are lined with windows, brightening the U-shaped kitchen. A butler's pantry leads past an interior foyer to the vaulted dining room and living room, separated by a two-way fireplace. To the rear, the master suite is replete with amenities, including a vaulted ceiling, innovative bath and rear property access. Upstairs, two bedrooms share a full bath and a sitting area, perfect for studying.

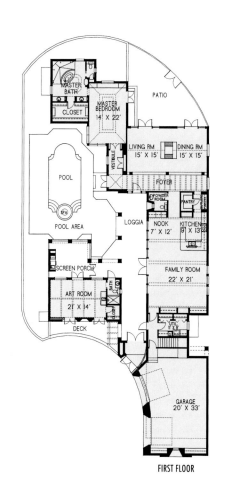

FIRST FLOOR

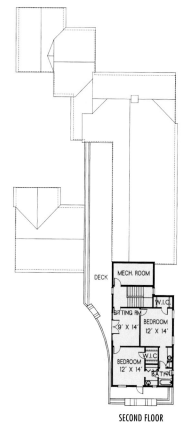

SECOND FLOOR

If you're dreaming of a traditional Spanish Colonial home with historic detail, yet all the modern amenities of today's homes, you are in luck! This amazing design will be a neighborhood showpiece and a comfortable place to call your own. Upon entry, the foyer opens to the two-story great room, with a warming fireplace and sweeping vistas. A gourmet island kitchen is just the thing for preparing quick snacks and elegant feasts. For the family who loves to entertain, turn the octagonal den into a banquet dining room. The left wing is devoted to the master suite; a grand bedroom, lavish bath and private study access through the generous walk-in closet make it a true haven. Upper-level bedrooms share a full bath and rear balcony access.

plan# HPT810071

STYLE: SPANISH COLONIAL
FIRST FLOOR: 2,417 SQ. FT.
SECOND FLOOR: 595 SQ. FT.
TOTAL: 3,012 SQ. FT.
BEDROOMS: 3
BATHROOMS: 2½
WIDTH: 57'-4"
DEPTH: 86'-9"
FOUNDATION: SLAB

SEARCH ONLINE @ EPLANS.COM

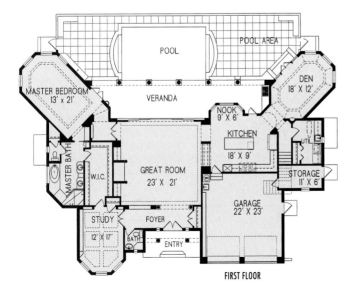

FIRST FLOOR

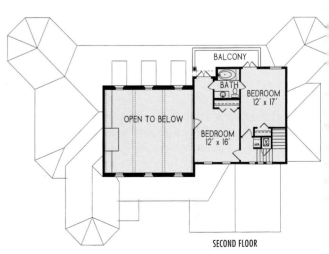

SECOND FLOOR

TO ORDER BLUEPRINTS CALL TOLL FREE 1-800-521-679

plan# HPT810072

STYLE: SPANISH COLONIAL
SQUARE FOOTAGE: 3,596
BONUS SPACE: 444 SQ. FT.
BEDROOMS: 3
BATHROOMS: 2½ + ½
WIDTH: 97'-0"
DEPTH: 140'-6"
FOUNDATION: SLAB

SEARCH ONLINE @ EPLANS.COM

What do you get when you cross a traditional family home with a Spanish Colonial villa? Everything! This outstanding plan is suited to any neighborhood, yet retains a strong Southwestern presence. A textured stucco entry reveals a lush courtyard. To the right, two family bedrooms and a study enjoy privacy and quiet. A vintage-style beamed ceiling continues from the great room and dining room into the island kitchen. The secluded master suite celebrates luxury with a sitting room, private veranda, exercise area and resplendent bath. A bonus room above the three-car garage provides space for a guest suite. Not to be missed: expanded courtyard/veranda areas and a cabana with a separate bath and outdoor fireplace.

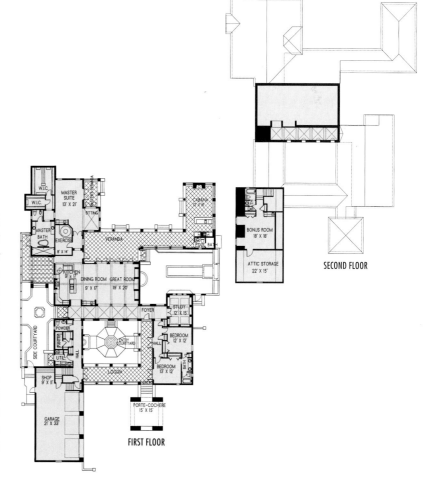

SECOND FLOOR

FIRST FLOOR

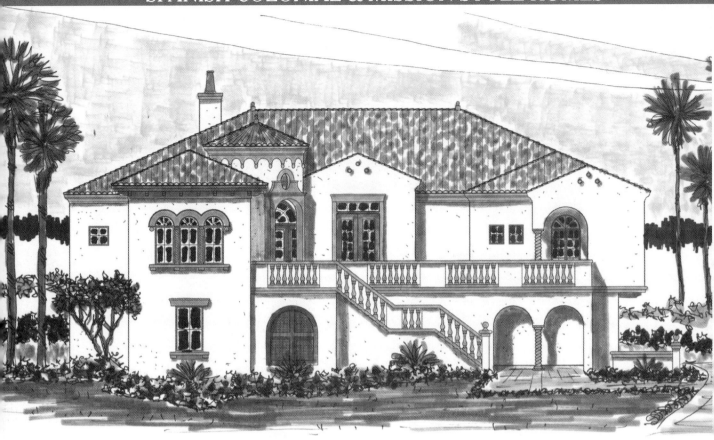

Looking a bit like a villa resort, this breathtaking Spanish Colonial beauty is designed to pamper every member of the family. Enter from the upper-level, or take the garage elevator—great for heavy loads of groceries. The foyer reveals an elegant dining room and unique great room, each with outdoor access. An angled kitchen opens to the bright breakfast nook, and is equipped with both a butler's and walk-in pantry. Two bedrooms to the right enjoy private baths. In the left wing, the master suite opens through French doors; past the extra storage closet, the bedroom is bathed in natural light, courtesy of sliding glass doors. An immense walk-in closet and decadent bath with a corner whirlpool tub are wonderful additions. A nearby study is accented with arched windows.

plan# HPT810073

STYLE: SPANISH COLONIAL
SQUARE FOOTAGE: 2,846
BEDROOMS: 3
BATHROOMS: 3½
WIDTH: 66'-8"
DEPTH: 91'-4"
FOUNDATION: PIER

SEARCH ONLINE @ EPLANS.COM

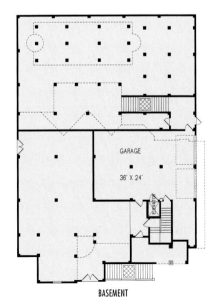

BASEMENT

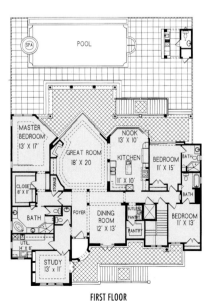

FIRST FLOOR

plan# HPT810074

STYLE: SPANISH COLONIAL
LOWER LEVEL: 929 SQ. FT.
MAIN LEVEL: 2,092 SQ. FT.
UPPER LEVEL: 2,437 SQ. FT.
TOTAL: 5,458 SQ. FT.
BEDROOMS: 7
BATHROOMS: 7½
WIDTH: 74'-10"
DEPTH: 75'-2"
FOUNDATION: SLAB

SEARCH ONLINE @ EPLANS.COM

This captivating Spanish Colonial villa includes three levels of living space to accommodate seven bedrooms and seven full baths—an elevator accesses every level. Enter on the ground floor to find a game room, guest suite and pool area. Upstairs, the main level supports a comfortable living room, with a cozy fireplace and French doors to the balcony. The kitchen opens to a nook, bathed in light. Three family bedrooms and a guest suite—each with private baths—complete the level. One more flight of stairs leads to the upper living areas, comprising an inviting family room, formal dining room and ancillary kitchen, private study, and two bedrooms. The master suite is a decadent retreat, with two private balconies, a fireplace-warmed bath, recessed whirlpool tub, and a compartmented toilet and bidet.

LOWER LEVEL

MAIN LEVEL

UPPER LEVEL

This delightful Spanish design will fit in well, regardless of your building location: mountains, endless prairie, farmland or suburbs. The hub of the plan is the kitchen/family room area. The beam ceiling and the raised-hearth fireplace contribute to the cozy, informal atmosphere. The living and dining rooms provide a great formal gathering spot. The master bedroom provides privacy from the three family bedrooms located at the opposite end of the plan. It features a magnificent view to the rear terrace and the landscape beyond.

plan⊕ HPT810075

STYLE: SPANISH COLONIAL
SQUARE FOOTAGE: 2,307
BEDROOMS: 4
BATHROOMS: 2
WIDTH: 70'-0"
DEPTH: 56'-0"
FOUNDATION: SLAB

SEARCH ONLINE @ EPLANS.COM

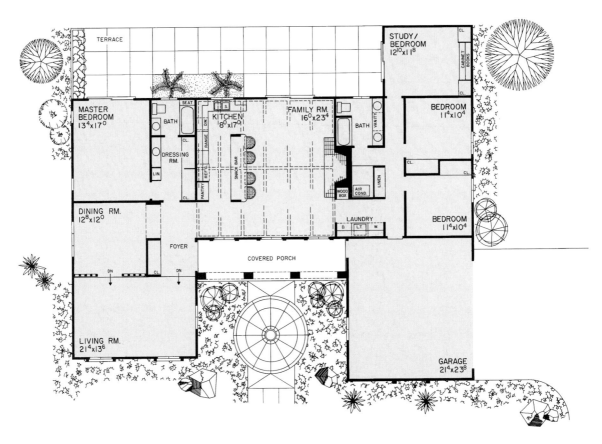

plan# HPT810076

L

STYLE: SPANISH
SQUARE FOOTAGE: 2,831
BEDROOMS: 4
BATHROOMS: 3
WIDTH: 84'-0"
DEPTH: 77'-0"
FOUNDATION: SLAB

SEARCH ONLINE @ EPLANS.COM

QUOTE ONE®

Cost to build? See page 182
to order complete cost estimate
to build this house in your area!

Besides great curb appeal, this home has a wonderful floor plan. The foyer features a fountain that greets visitors and leads to a formal dining room on the right and a living room on the left. A large family room at the rear has a built-in entertainment center and a fireplace. The U-shaped kitchen is perfectly located for servicing all living and dining areas. To the right of the plan, away from the central entertaining spaces, are three family bedrooms sharing a full bath. On the left side, with solitude and comfort for the master suite, are a large sitting area, an office and an amenity-filled bath. A deck with a spa sits outside the master suite.

A majestic facade makes this home pleasing to view. This home provides dual-use space in the wonderful sunken sitting room and media area. The kitchen has a breakfast bay and overlooks the snack bar to the sunken family area. A few steps from the kitchen is the formal dining room, which functions well with the upper patio. Two family bedrooms share a full bath. The private master suite includes a sitting area and French doors that open to a private covered patio.

plan# HPT810077

STYLE: SPANISH
SQUARE FOOTAGE: 2,086
BEDROOMS: 3
BATHROOMS: 2
WIDTH: 82'-0"
DEPTH: 58'-4"
FOUNDATION: SLAB

SEARCH ONLINE @ EPLANS.COM

QUOTE ONE®
Cost to build? See page 182
to order complete cost estimate
to build this house in your area!

plan⊕ HPT810078

L

STYLE: MISSION
SQUARE FOOTAGE: 2,612
BEDROOMS: 4
BATHROOMS: 2½
WIDTH: 93'-7"
DEPTH: 74'-10"
FOUNDATION: SLAB

SEARCH ONLINE @ EPLANS.COM

ramatic interior angles provide for
immensely livable plan that is metered
ith elegance enough for any social occa-
on. The open passage to the living room
d formal dining room from the foyer is
erfect for entertaining, while casual areas
e positioned to the rear of the plan. The
acious kitchen, with extra storage at
ery turn, has an eat-in nook and a door to
e rear patio. Two family bedrooms share a
ll bath to complete this wing. The master
ite is split from the family area to ensure
private retreat. The large bedroom can
sily accommodate a sitting area and has a
xurious bath, walk-in closet and sliding
ors to a private patio.

QUOTE ONE®

Cost to build? See page 182
to order complete cost estimate
to build this house in your area!

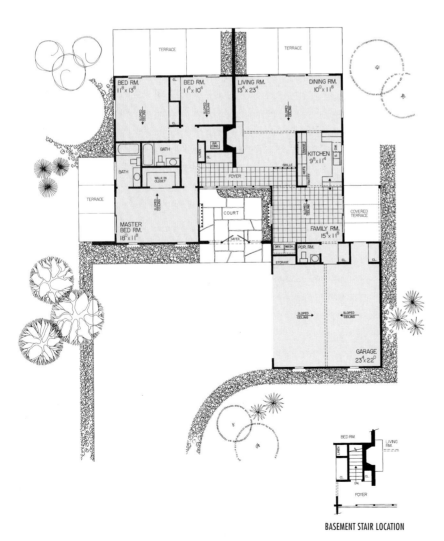

BASEMENT STAIR LOCATION

plan# HPT810079

STYLE: SPANISH COLONIAL
SQUARE FOOTAGE: 1,695
BEDROOMS: 3
BATHROOMS: 2½
WIDTH: 63'-8"
DEPTH: 62'-8"
FOUNDATION: SLAB

SEARCH ONLINE @ EPLANS.COM

This petite Spanish Colonial desig
packs a lot of living space into its 1,695 squa
feet. An entry courtyard opens to a tiled foye
to the right, the family room—also with a ti
floor—includes sliding glass doors that ope
to a side terrace. The efficient galley kitch
serves the living/dining area with ease. Thre
bedrooms—a master suite and two seconda
bedrooms—reside to the left of the plan. Th
master suite features a private bath, walk-
closet and access to a private side terrace; tw
additional bedrooms open to the rear terrac

plan# HPT810080

STYLE: SPANISH COLONIAL
SQUARE FOOTAGE: 2,341
BONUS SPACE: 1,380 SQ. FT.
BEDROOMS: 4
BATHROOMS: 3½
WIDTH: 66'-0"
DEPTH: 66'-0"
FOUNDATION: BASEMENT

SEARCH ONLINE @ EPLANS.COM

The street view of this contemporary Spanish-style home shows a beautifully designed one-story home, but take a look at the rear elevation. This home has been designed to be built into a hill, so the lower level is open to the sunlight. With an abundance of casual living space on the lower level, including a games room, full bath, a lounge with a fireplace and even a summer kitchen with a full-sized snack bar, the formal living space can be reserved for the main floor—or leave this space for future expansion. From the foyer, the formal living room and dining room take center stage. The large kitchen has an angled snack bar that is open to the family room. The master suite has a covered porch and split-vanity bath. Two family bedrooms share a full hall bath.

BASEMENT

FIRST FLOOR

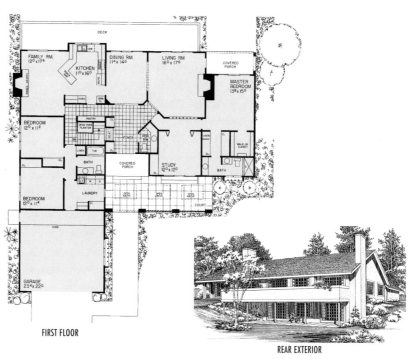

REAR EXTERIOR

The entry court of this design features planter areas and a small pool. Down six steps from the foyer is the lower level, housing a bedroom and full bath, a study and an activities room. Upper-level sleeping quarters are located six steps up from the foyer. The main level accommodates the living areas: formal living room, kitchen and adjoining breakfast room, powder room and laundry room. A three-car garage allows plenty of room for the family fleet.

plan# HPT810081

L D

STYLE: SPANISH COLONIAL
MAIN LEVEL: 1,530 SQ. FT.
UPPER LEVEL: 984 SQ. FT.
LOWER LEVEL: 3,465 SQ. FT.
BEDROOMS: 4
BATHROOMS: 3½
WIDTH: 90'-0"
DEPTH: 56'-0"
FOUNDATION: BASEMENT

SEARCH ONLINE @ EPLANS.COM

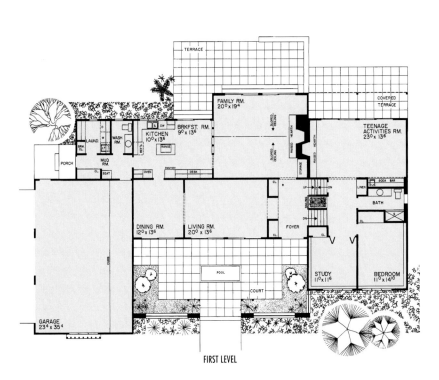

FIRST LEVEL

UPPER LEVEL

QUOTE ON
Cost to build? See page 182
to order complete cost estim
to build this house in your

plan# HPT810082

L D

STYLE: SPANISH
FIRST FLOOR: 2,121 SQ. FT.
SECOND FLOOR: 913 SQ. FT.
TOTAL: 3,034 SQ. FT.
BEDROOMS: 4
BATHROOMS: 2½
WIDTH: 84'-0"
DEPTH: 48'-0"
FOUNDATION: BASEMENT

SEARCH ONLINE @ EPLANS.COM

This striking contemporary design with Spanish good looks offers outstanding livability for today's active lifestyles. A three-car garage leads to a mudroom, laundry and washroom. An efficient, spacious kitchen opens to a large dining room, with a pass-through also leading to the family room. This room and the adjoining master bedroom suite overlook a backyard terrace. Just off the master bedroom is a sizable study that opens to a foyer. Stairs just off the foyer make upstairs access quick and easy. The hub of this terrific plan is a living room that faces the front courtyard. Upstairs, three family bedrooms share a bath and the spacious lounge.

SECOND FLOOR

FIRST FLOOR

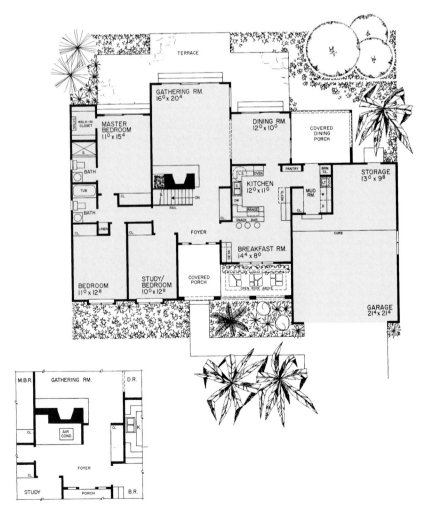

OPTIONAL LAYOUT

plan# HPT810083

LD

STYLE: SPANISH COLONIAL
SQUARE FOOTAGE: 1,674
BEDROOMS: 3
BATHROOMS: 2
WIDTH: 68'-0"
DEPTH: 48'-8"
FOUNDATION: BASEMENT

SEARCH ONLINE @ EPLANS.COM

Stucco arches, multi-paned windows and a gracefully sloped roof accent the exterior of this Spanish-inspired design. The front foyer leads to each of the living areas: a sloped-ceiling gathering room, a study (or optional bedroom), a formal dining room and the light-filled breakfast room. Bedrooms are in a wing to the left and feature a master suite with a walk-in closet and terrace access. A covered porch opens off the dining room for private outdoor meals. The two-car garage is made even more useful with a large storage area—or use it for workshop space.

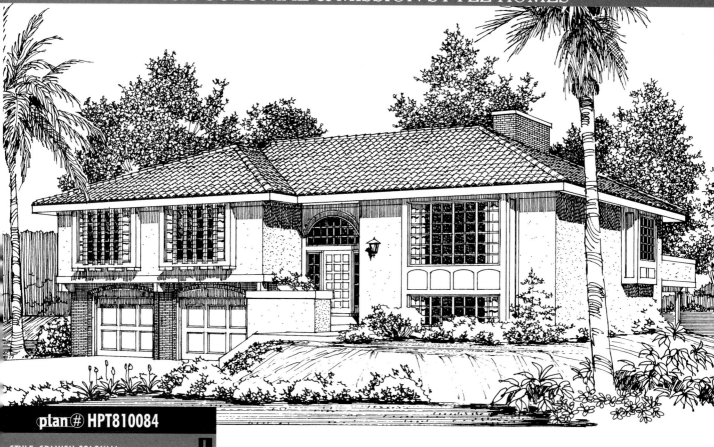

plan# HPT810084

L

STYLE: SPANISH COLONIAL
FIRST FLOOR: 1,181 SQ. FT.
SECOND FLOOR: 1,861 SQ. FT.
TOTAL: 3,042 SQ. FT.
BEDROOMS: 4
BATHROOMS: 3
WIDTH: 54'-0"
DEPTH: 40'-4"
FOUNDATION: BASEMENT

SEARCH ONLINE @ EPLANS.COM

A Spanish-style split-level? Why not? This one has lots going for it upstairs and down. Up top, note the living room and formal dining room; they share a fireplace, and each leads to a cozy deck out back. In addition, the kitchen and breakfast area are centers of attention; the latter has a wonderful oversized pantry. Zoned to the left of the entry are three bedrooms (two if you make one a study). Down below is a potpourri of space: family room, lounge with raised-hearth fireplace, large laundry room (note the bay window), another bedroom, full bath and plenty of storage in the garage.

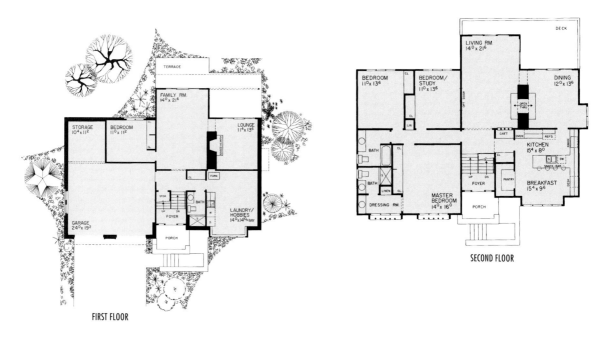

FIRST FLOOR

SECOND FLOOR

Here, the Spanish Southwest comes to life in the form of an enchanting multi-level home, with grand architectural detailing. The entrance courtyard, the twin balconies and the roof treatment are particularly noteworthy. At the rear of the house are the covered patio and the balcony with its lower patio. The upper level has three bedrooms and two baths; the main level has formal living and dining rooms to the rear and a kitchen area looking onto the courtyard; the lower level features the family room, study and laundry. There are two fireplaces—each with a raised hearth.

plan⊕ HPT810085

STYLE: SPANISH COLONIAL
MAIN LEVEL: 832 SQ. FT.
UPPER LEVEL: 864 SQ. FT.
LOWER LEVEL: 864 SQ. FT.
TOTAL: 2,560 SQ. FT.
BEDROOMS: 3
BATHROOMS: 3½
WIDTH: 80'-0"
DEPTH: 48'-0"
FOUNDATION: SLAB

SEARCH ONLINE @ EPLANS.COM

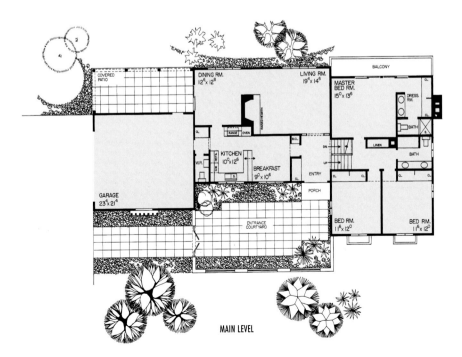

MAIN LEVEL

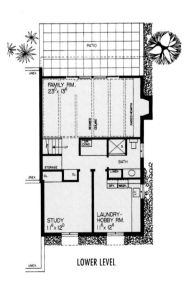

LOWER LEVEL

TO ORDER BLUEPRINTS CALL TOLL FREE 1-800-521-679

plan# HPT810086

L D

STYLE: SPANISH
SQUARE FOOTAGE: 2,261
BEDROOMS: 4
BATHROOMS: 2½
WIDTH: 85'-8"
DEPTH: 46'-0"
FOUNDATION: BASEMENT

SEARCH ONLINE @ EPLANS.COM

A privacy wall around the courtyard, with a pool and trellised planter area, is a gracious way to enter this one-story design. The Spanish flavor is accented by the grillwork and the tiled roof. The front living room has sliding glass doors, which open to the entrance court. The adjacent dining room features a bay window. Informal activities will be enjoyed in the rear family room with a sloped, beamed ceiling, a raised-hearth fireplace, sliding glass doors to the terrace and a snack bar. The sleeping wing can remain quiet away from the plan's activity centers. Notice the three-car garage with extra storage space.

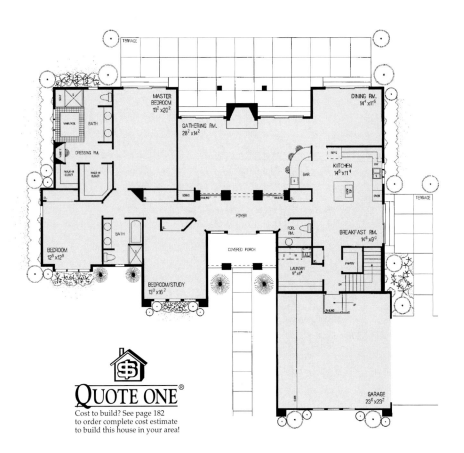

Quote One®

Cost to build? See page 182
to order complete cost estimate
to build this house in your area!

plan# HPT810087

STYLE: SPANISH
SQUARE FOOTAGE: 2,559
BEDROOMS: 3
BATHROOMS: 2½
WIDTH: 74'-0"
DEPTH: 66'-10"
FOUNDATION: BASEMENT

SEARCH ONLINE @ EPLANS.COM

A natural desert dweller, this stucco tile-roofed beauty is equally comfortable in any climate. Inside, there's a well-planned design. Common living areas—the gathering room, formal dining room and breakfast room—are offset by a quiet study that could be used as a bedroom or guest room. A master suite features two walk-in closets, a double vanity and whirlpool spa. The two-car garage provides a service entrance; close by is a laundry area and a pantry. A lovely hearth warms the gathering room and complements the snack bar.

plan# HPT810088

L

STYLE: SPANISH
FIRST FLOOR: 3,058 SQ. FT.
SECOND FLOOR: 279 SQ. FT.
TOTAL: 3,337 SQ. FT.
BEDROOMS: 4
BATHROOMS: 2½
WIDTH: 104'-6"
DEPTH: 58'-4"
FOUNDATION: SLAB

SEARCH ONLINE @ EPLANS.COM

A centrally located interior atrium is just one of the interesting features of this Spanish design. The atrium has a built-in seat and will bring light to the adjacent living room, dining room and breakfast room. Beyond the foyer and down one step, a tiled reception hall includes a powder room. This area leads to the sleeping wing and up one step to the family room with its raised-hearth fireplace and sliding glass doors to the rear terrace. Overlooking the family room is a railed lounge that can be used for various activities. Sleeping areas include a deluxe master suite and three family bedrooms.

Quote ONE®
Cost to build? See page 182
to order complete cost estimate
to build this house in your area!

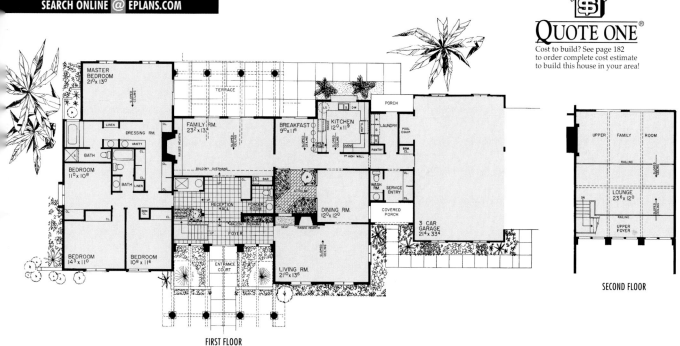

FIRST FLOOR

SECOND FLOOR

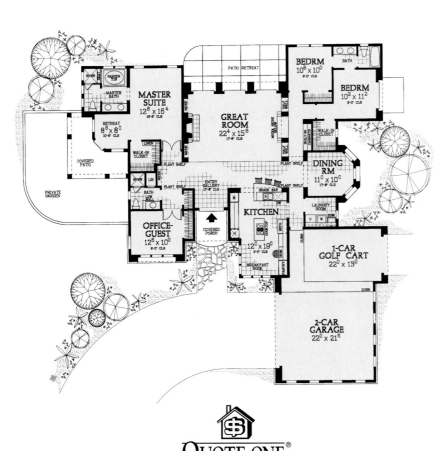

Quote One®

Cost to build? See page 182
to order complete cost estimate
to build this house in your area!

plan# HPT810089

STYLE: MISSION
SQUARE FOOTAGE: 2,385
BEDROOMS: 4
BATHROOMS: 2½
WIDTH: 76'-6"
DEPTH: 77'-4"
FOUNDATION: SLAB

SEARCH ONLINE @ EPLANS.COM

A vaulted entry and tall muntin windows complement a classic stucco exterior on this Mission-style home. Inside, an entry gallery opens to a great room, which offers generous views to the rear property and columned access to a patio retreat. Niches, built-ins and half-walls decorate and help define this area. The nearby kitchen features an island cooktop counter and a cozy snack bar. The formal dining room offers privacy and natural light from a bay window. A secluded master wing soothes with a sumptuous bath, walk-in closet and an inner retreat with access to a covered patio. A nearby office with triple windows could also accommodate guests.

plan# HPT810090

L

STYLE: MISSION
SQUARE FOOTAGE: 2,573
BEDROOMS: 3
BATHROOMS: 2½
WIDTH: 94'-6"
DEPTH: 79'-11"
FOUNDATION: SLAB

SEARCH ONLINE @ EPLANS.COM

An expansive living room/dining area in this design makes a grand impression. The kitchen includes a large pantry and an adjoining breakfast nook with access to a family entertainment patio. A courtyard in the front can be reached through the dining room or the front bedroom. Both the family and living rooms offer fireplaces. Each of the bedrooms includes a walk-in closet and convenient access to a full bath.

QUOTE ONE®
Cost to build? See page 182
to order complete cost estimate
to build this house in your area!

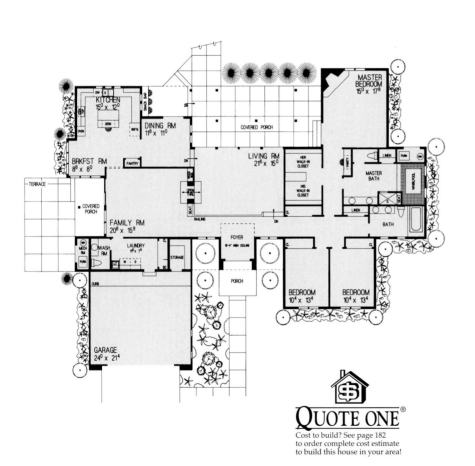

QUOTE ONE ®

Cost to build? See page 182
to order complete cost estimate
to build this house in your area!

plan # HPT810091

STYLE: SPANISH COLONIAL
SQUARE FOOTAGE: 2,850
BEDROOMS: 3
BATHROOMS: 2½
WIDTH: 86'-0"
DEPTH: 69'-0"
FOUNDATION: SLAB

SEARCH ONLINE @ EPLANS.COM

This Southwestern design cater
to families who enjoy outdoor living an
entertaining. Doors open onto a shade
terrace from the master bedroom an
living room, while a sliding glass door i
the family room accesses a smaller te
race. Outdoor entertaining is a breez
with the outdoor bar with pass-throug
window to the kitchen. In the sleepin
wing, two secondary bedrooms share
hall bath with a dual-bowl vanity; th
master suite is designed to pamper th
fortunate homeowner with such amen
ties as a corner fireplace, His and He
walk-in closets, a whirlpool tub, a sep
rate shower and a separate vanity.

plan# HPT810092

L

STYLE: MISSION
FIRST FLOOR: 1,522 SQ. FT.
SECOND FLOOR: 800 SQ. FT.
TOTAL: 2,322 SQ. FT.
BEDROOMS: 4
BATHROOMS: 3½
WIDTH: 69'-6"
DEPTH: 56'-0"
FOUNDATION: SLAB

SEARCH ONLINE @ EPLANS.COM

QUOTE ONE®

Cost to build? See page 182
to order complete cost estimate
to build this house in your area!

SECOND FLOOR

FIRST FLOOR

This two-story Spanish Mission-
style home has character inside and out.
The first-floor master suite features a fireplace and gracious bath with a walk-in
closet, a whirlpool, a shower, dual vanities
and linen storage. A second fireplace
serves both the gathering room and
media room/library. The kitchen, with an
island cooktop, includes a snack bar and
an adjoining breakfast nook. Three bedrooms—one a wonderful guest suite—and
two full baths occupy the second floor.

SECOND FLOOR

Quote One®

Cost to build? See page 182
to order complete cost estimate
to build this house in your area!

plan # HPT810093

STYLE: MISSION
FIRST FLOOR: 1,946 SQ. FT.
SECOND FLOOR: 986 SQ. FT.
TOTAL: 2,932 SQ. FT.
BEDROOMS: 4
BATHROOMS: 3½
WIDTH: 89'-0"
DEPTH: 56'-0"
FOUNDATION: SLAB

SEARCH ONLINE @ EPLANS.COM

Here's a grand Spanish Mission
home designed for family living. Enter at the
angled foyer which contains a curved staircase to the second floor. Family bedrooms are
here along with a spacious guest suite. The
master bedroom is found on the first floor and
has a private patio and whirlpool tub, both
overlooking an enclosed garden area. In addition to the living room and dining room connected by a through-fireplace, there is a family
room with casual eating space. The spacious
library features a large closet. You'll appre-
ciate the abundant built-ins and unique
shapes throughout this home.

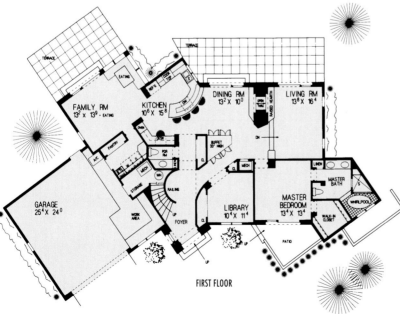

FIRST FLOOR

plan# HPT810094

L

STYLE: MISSION
SQUARE FOOTAGE: 2,966
BEDROOMS: 4
BATHROOMS: 3½
WIDTH: 114'-10"
DEPTH: 79'-2"
FOUNDATION: SLAB

SEARCH ONLINE @ EPLANS.COM

The dramatic entrance of this grand Southwestern home gives way to interesting angles and optimum livability inside. Columns frame the formal living room, which provides views of the rear grounds from the foyer. The private master bedroom is contained on the left portion of the plan. Here, a relaxing master bath provides an abundance of amenities that include a walk-in closet, a bumped-out whirlpool tub, a separate shower and a double-bowl vanity. A clutter room and powder room complete this wing. Centrally located for efficiency, the kitchen easily serves the living room—via a pass-through—as well as the formal dining room, family room and flex room. Three secondary bedrooms share two full baths.

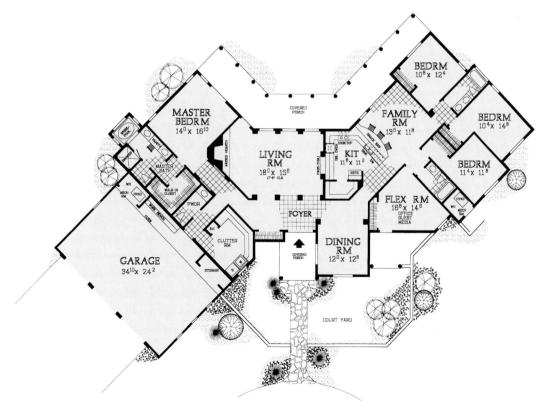

A grand entry enhances the exterior of this elegant stucco home. The office located at the front of the plan makes this design ideal for a home-based business. Formal areas combine to provide lots of space for entertaining. The kitchen, complete with a snack bar and a breakfast nook, opens to the family room, which connects to the media room. The private master suite includes two retreats—one is a multi-windowed sitting area, the other contains a spa for outdoor enjoyment. A walk-in closet and a luxurious bath complete this area. Two family bedrooms share a full bath.

plan# HPT810095

STYLE: MISSION
SQUARE FOOTAGE: 3,034
BEDROOMS: 3
BATHROOMS: 3
WIDTH: 112'-0"
DEPTH: 74'-6"
FOUNDATION: SLAB

SEARCH ONLINE @ EPLANS.COM

QUOTE ONE®

Cost to build? See page 182 to order complete cost estimate to build this house in your area!

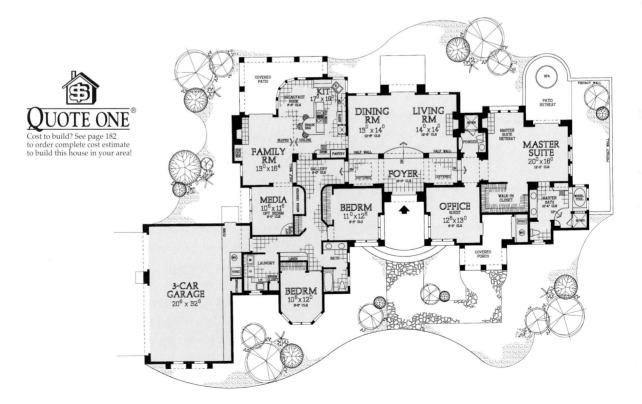

plan # HPT810096

STYLE: MISSION
FIRST FLOOR: 1,731 SQ. FT.
SECOND FLOOR: 554 SQ. FT.
TOTAL: 2,285 SQ. FT.
BEDROOMS: 3
BATHROOMS: 2½
WIDTH: 90'-2"
DEPTH: 69'-10"
FOUNDATION: SLAB

SEARCH ONLINE @ EPLANS.COM

QUOTE ONE®
Cost to build? See page 182
to order complete cost estimate
to build this house in your area!

SECOND FLOOR

FIRST FLOOR

arying roof planes of colorful tile surfaces help
make a dramatic statement on this elegant design.
rivacy walls add appeal and help form the front court-
rd and side private patio. The kitchen has an island
oktop, built-in ovens, a nearby walk-in pantry and
rect access to the outdoor covered patio. The living
om is impressive with its centered fireplace with long,
ised hearth and access through French doors to the
ar patio. At the opposite end of the plan is the master
droom. It has a walk-in closet with shoe storage, dual
nities in the bath, plus a whirlpool and stall shower.
e two secondary bedrooms upstairs have direct
cess to a bath with twin sinks. There is also a loft with
en rail overlooking the curved stairway.

plan# HPT810097

STYLE: SPANISH COLONIAL
SQUARE FOOTAGE: 3,212
BEDROOMS: 3
BATHROOMS: 2½
WIDTH: 108'-0"
DEPTH: 57'-0"
FOUNDATION: SLAB

SEARCH ONLINE @ EPLANS.COM

This one-story home pairs the customary tile and stucco of Spanish design with a very livable floor plan. The sunken living room with its open-hearth fireplace promises to be a cozy gathering place. For more casual occasions, there's a welcoming family room with a fireplace off the foyer. The kitchen works well with the formal dining room and nearby breakfast room, which offers access to the rear terrace. Two secondary bedrooms share a large full hall bath while a sumptuous master suite enjoys a huge walk-in closet, a whirlpool tub, a separate shower and a romantic fireplace.

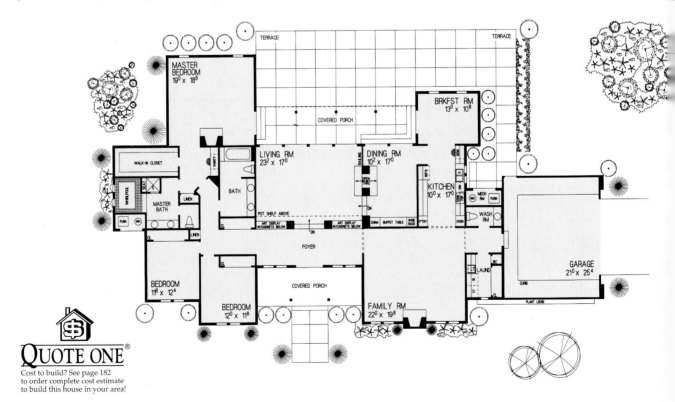

QUOTE ONE®
Cost to build? See page 182
to order complete cost estimate
to build this house in your area!

CONTEMPORARY SOUTHWESTERN HOMES

With a large entry courtyard and two outdoor fireplaces, this plan would be at home in any southwestern neighborhood.
Plan HPT810111; see page 165 for details.

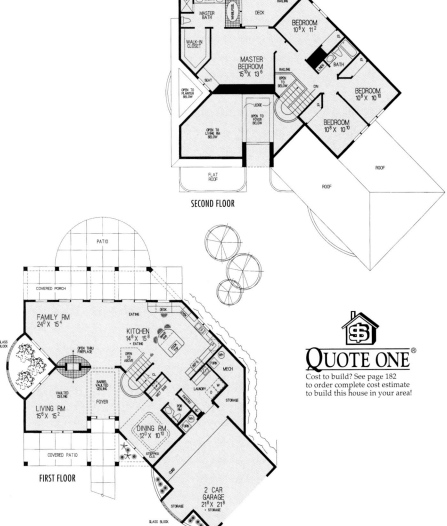

SECOND FLOOR

FIRST FLOOR

plan⊕ **HPT810098**

L

STYLE: SW CONTEMPORARY
FIRST FLOOR: 1,481 SQ. FT.
SECOND FLOOR: 1,287 SQ. FT.
TOTAL: 2,768 SQ. FT.
BEDROOMS: 4
BATHROOMS: 2½
WIDTH: 64'-0"
DEPTH: 56'-2"
FOUNDATION: SLAB

SEARCH ONLINE @ EPLANS.COM

QUOTE ONE®
Cost to build? See page 182
to order complete cost estimate
to build this house in your area!

Glass-block walls and a foyer with a barrel-vaulted ceiling create an interesting exterior on this contemporary Southwestern home. Covered porches to the front and rear provide for excellent indoor/outdoor living relationships. Inside, a large planter and through-fireplace enhance the living room and family room. A desk, eating area and snack bar are special features in the kitchen. The master suite is highlighted by a large walk-in closet, a bath with a separate shower and tub, and a private deck.

plan # HPT810099

STYLE: SW CONTEMPORARY
SQUARE FOOTAGE: 1,515
BEDROOMS: 3
BATHROOMS: 2
WIDTH: 58'-0"
DEPTH: 59'-4"
FOUNDATION: SLAB

SEARCH ONLINE @ EPLANS.COM

Traditional Southwestern style shines through on this charming three-bedroom home. From the covered entry, the foyer presents a vaulted great room, complete with amazing rear vistas. The vault continues to the galley kitchen and bayed breakfast nook, enhanced by floods of natural light. In the right wing, the master suite revels in a pampering whirlpool bath and access to the lanai—over 400 square feet of outdoor relaxation. Two additional bedrooms are located on the far left and share a full bath.

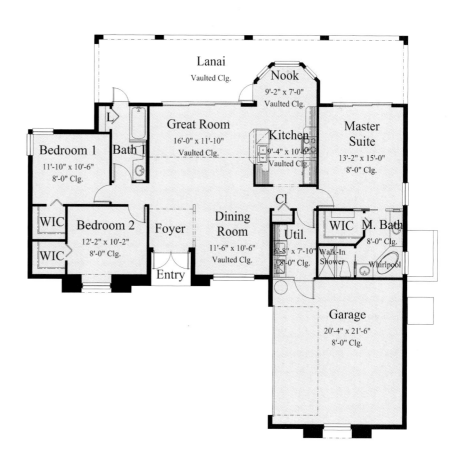

plan⊕ HPT810100

STYLE: SW CONTEMPORARY
SQUARE FOOTAGE: 2,407
BEDROOMS: 3
BATHROOMS: 2½
WIDTH: 72'-0"
DEPTH: 72'-0"
FOUNDATION: SLAB

SEARCH ONLINE @ EPLANS.COM

With clean lines, a tiled roof and multi-windowed portico, this one-story contemporary home possesses plenty of curb appeal. Inside, the living/dining area is flooded with light from two walls of windows and French-door access to the spacious courtyard. Located in the left wing, the living area includes a U-shaped kitchen with a huge walk-in pantry, breakfast area and large great room with a fireplace. To the right of the foyer is the sleeping wing. Here, a deluxe master bedroom features two walk-in closets, a round tub and access to the courtyard. Two secondary bedrooms share a hall bath.

plan# HPT810101

STYLE: SW CONTEMPORARY
FIRST FLOOR: 1,836 SQ. FT.
SECOND FLOOR: 575 SQ. FT.
TOTAL: 2,411 SQ. FT.
BEDROOMS: 3
BATHROOMS: 2½
WIDTH: 67'-4"
DEPTH: 72'-4"
FOUNDATION: SLAB

SEARCH ONLINE @ EPLANS.COM

Smooth lines, many windows and an impressive entrance mark this home as contemporary. Inside, the lavish master suite boasts two walk-in closets and a sumptuous bath with courtyard access. The open living/dining area offers a fireplace. An angled kitchen features a snack bar that serves the adjacent great room. Two options are supplied for the second floor—one offers three bedrooms and a hall bath, while the other has two bedrooms, a large bath and access to a deck.

SECOND FLOOR

ALTERNATE SECOND FLOOR

FIRST FLOOR

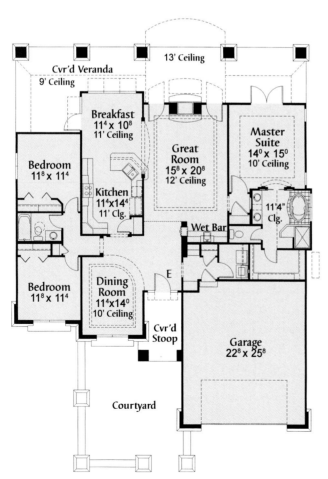

plan # HPT810102

STYLE: SW CONTEMPORARY
SQUARE FOOTAGE: 1,949
BEDROOMS: 3
BATHROOMS: 2
WIDTH: 56'-0"
DEPTH: 69'-4"
FOUNDATION: SLAB

SEARCH ONLINE @ EPLANS.COM

Wide wall bases provide a sturdy appearance to this modern Southwestern home. Inside, the dining room is located off the entry, defined by a rounded tray ceiling. Just ahead, a large modified-galley kitchen serves the breakfast nook with ease; a serving counter overlooks the great room's striking fireplace. A wet bar is an added benefit, great for entertaining. The nearby master suite enjoys French door veranda access and a vaulted bath. Two additional bedrooms share a hall bath to the left of the plan.

Don't be fooled by appearances!

Although this Southwestern-inspired home looks like a traditional family design, the floor plan is anything but ordinary. Raised ceilings in nearly every room create a feeling of spaciousness, and personal touches abound. The entry gives way to a formal dining room. Located for convenience, a China hutch and buffet niche are just ahead. The wet bar and island kitchen will entertain guests, as the great room invites gatherings by the fireplace. Each of the four bedrooms has private outdoor access; the master suite enjoys an exclusive patio (with a fireplace) and a lavish private bath.

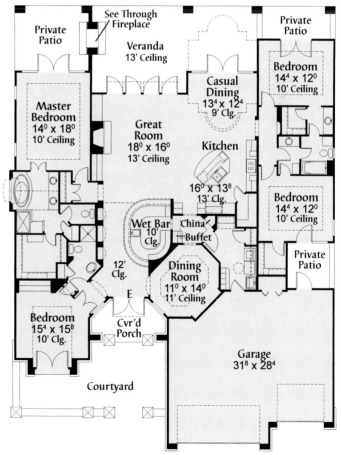

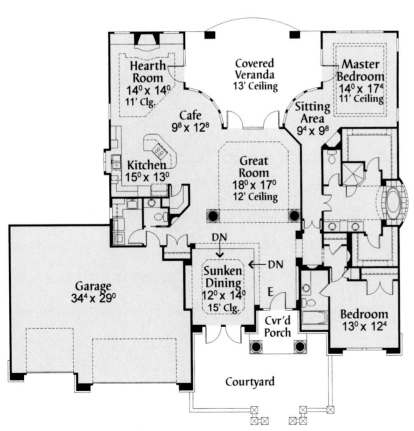

plan# HPT810104

STYLE: SW CONTEMPORARY
SQUARE FOOTAGE: 2,482
BEDROOMS: 2
BATHROOMS: 2½
WIDTH: 76'-8"
DEPTH: 66'-4"
FOUNDATION: SLAB

SEARCH ONLINE @ EPLANS.COM

This modern Southwestern home reflects a hint of the Mediterranean for fresh style and architectural interest. Enter through a well-lit foyer; on the left, a sunken dining room enjoys French doors to the front courtyard. Columns separate the great room, an ideal place for gatherings of any occasion. Completing the living areas, the island kitchen overlooks a bowed "cafe" and the cozy hearth room. The master suite begins with French doors and a gallery hall. A bowed sitting area and inset niche are a romantic touch. In the private bath, a spectacular spa tub invites hours of relaxation. An additional bedroom at the front of the home enjoys a private bath as well.

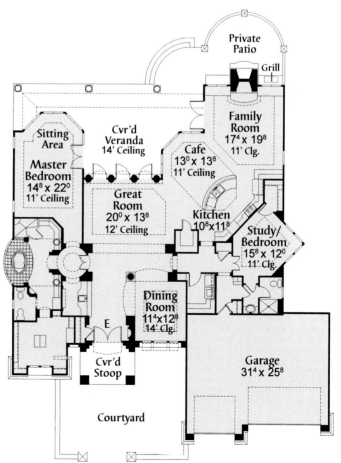

plan⊕ HPT810105

STYLE: SW CONTEMPORARY
SQUARE FOOTAGE: 2,720
BEDROOMS: 2
BATHROOMS: 2
WIDTH: 72'-10"
DEPTH: 79'-10"
FOUNDATION: SLAB

SEARCH ONLINE @ EPLANS.COM

Double doors provide an elegant entry to this contemporary Southwestern plan, which features a range of lavish amenities designed for today's active lifestyles. The dining room, brightened by a triple window and defined by a wide column, serves as a spot to host formal gatherings; for quieter family events, the family room and cafe area are tucked cozily to the rear of the plan. For outdoor entertaining, try the covered rear veranda—accessible from the great room, cafe and family room—with its fireplace and built-in grill. The master bedroom includes a bayed sitting area and a resplendent private bath; a secondary bedroom, located to the opposite side of the plan, features a walk-in closet and has access to a full hall bath.

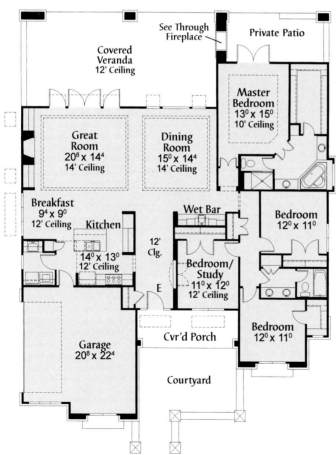

Covered Veranda
12' Ceiling

See Through Fireplace

Private Patio

Master Bedroom
13⁰ x 15⁰
10' Ceiling

Great Room
20⁸ x 14⁴
14' Ceiling

Dining Room
15⁰ x 14⁴
14' Ceiling

Breakfast
9⁴ x 9⁰
12' Ceiling

Kitchen
14⁰ x 13⁰
12' Ceiling

Wet Bar

Bedroom
12⁰ x 11⁰

12' Clg.

Bedroom/ Study
11⁰ x 12⁰
12' Ceiling

Garage
20⁸ x 22⁴

Cvr'd Porch

Bedroom
12⁰ x 11⁰

Courtyard

plan# HPT810106

STYLE: SW CONTEMPORARY
SQUARE FOOTAGE: 2,275
BEDROOMS: 4
BATHROOMS: 2
WIDTH: 58'-4"
DEPTH: 74'-0"
FOUNDATION: SLAB

SEARCH ONLINE @ EPLANS.COM

This ambitious contemporary design uses strong lines and graduated exterior walls fo a compelling presence in any neighborhood. Jus inside, optional French doors open to a quiet bed room or study. Follow the heightened entry to th great room and dining room, each topped by fourteen-foot tray ceiling. A nearby wet bar wi make anyone feel like an expert host. The kitche is hard working (so you can relax) with space fo a six-burner range, a dual-sink island, and an ef cient layout. To the right, a full bath serves th secondary bedrooms. The master suite expresse grandeur with a private hearth-warmed patio ar refined whirlpool bath.

TO ORDER BLUEPRINTS CALL TOLL FREE 1-800-521-679

plan# HPT810107

STYLE: SW CONTEMPORARY
SQUARE FOOTAGE: 2,120
BEDROOMS: 2
BATHROOMS: 2
WIDTH: 62'-8"
DEPTH: 82'-0"
FOUNDATION: SLAB

SEARCH ONLINE @ EPLANS.COM

The "new Southwest" is exemplified in this charming contemporary design. A half-walled courtyard ushers you to full-length glass doors; the entry presents a floor plan designed for entertaining. A formal dining room has a bumped-out niche, great for banquets. A china cabinet and built in buffet are conveniently nearby. A full wet bar has a rounded counter and overlooks the wall niches. In the great room, a fireplace framed by built-ins is viewed from the cooktop-island kitchen. A secluded master suite hosts a vaulted whirlpool bath and a private patio with a see-through fireplace. A splayed study/bedroom resides at the front of the home and accesses a full bath.

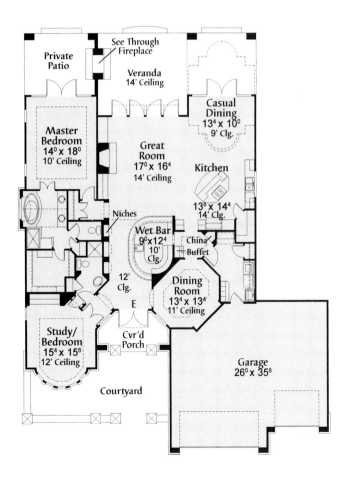

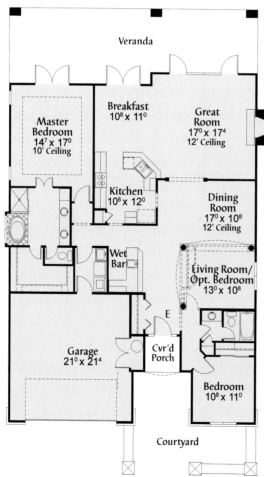

Veranda

Master Bedroom 14⁷ x 17⁰ 10' Ceiling

Breakfast 10⁸ x 11⁰

Great Room 17⁰ x 17⁴ 12' Ceiling

Kitchen 10⁸ x 12⁰

Dining Room 17⁰ x 10⁸ 12' Ceiling

Wet Bar

Living Room/ Opt. Bedroom 13⁰ x 10⁸

Garage 21⁰ x 21⁴

Cvr'd Porch

E

Bedroom 10⁸ x 11⁰

Courtyard

plan ⊕ HPT810108

STYLE: SW CONTEMPORARY
SQUARE FOOTAGE: 1,899
BEDROOMS: 3
BATHROOMS: 2
WIDTH: 46'-0"
DEPTH: 78'-2"
FOUNDATION: SLAB

SEARCH ONLINE @ EPLANS.COM

This petite Southwest design ideal for a narrow lot; inside, an inventiv floor plan makes the most of a small squar footage and brings family areas to life. Th entry opens to a columned living room on th right, or finish the space for an extra se ondary bedroom. Continue to find a centr kitchen, well-appointed and created to serv the dining room and breakfast nook. A nearb wet bar makes entertaining easy. The grea room makes a grand impression, balanced b a warming hearth. For quiet respite, th master suite excels, complete with Frenc doors and a refined spa bath. A two-ca garage offers a convenient service entranc

TO ORDER BLUEPRINTS CALL TOLL FREE 1-800-521-679

plan# HPT810109

STYLE: SW CONTEMPORARY
SQUARE FOOTAGE: 2,734
BEDROOMS: 4
BATHROOMS: 3
WIDTH: 63'-6"
DEPTH: 78'-4"
FOUNDATION: SLAB

SEARCH ONLINE @ EPLANS.COM

Bold lines and contemporary features celebrate a Southwestern spirit on this enchanting design. A grand entry reveals a living room on the right. Ahead, a tray ceiling defines a flexible area, perfect as a parlor or receiving area. A uniquely shaped island and immense walk-in pantry in the kitchen will please any chef; open planning affords views of the remarkable two-way fireplace in the gathering room. A formal dining room is sized for banquets. The master suite revels in a sunny sitting room and a dazzling private bath.

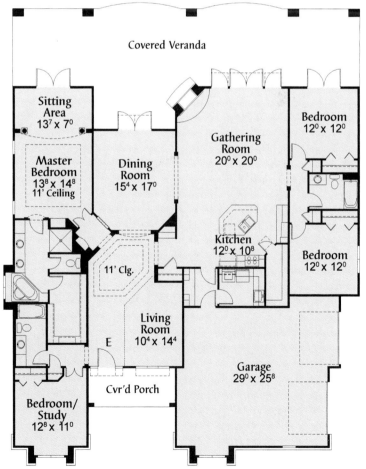

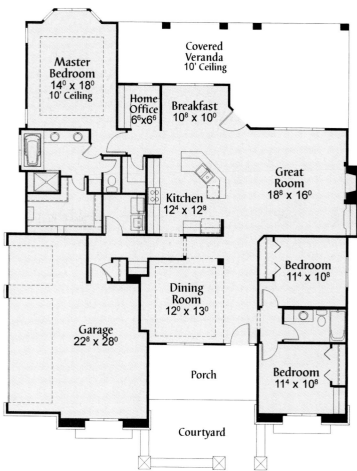

Master Bedroom 14⁰ x 18⁰ 10' Ceiling

Covered Veranda 10' Ceiling

Home Office 6⁶x6⁶

Breakfast 10⁸ x 10⁰

Great Room 18⁸ x 16⁰

Kitchen 12⁴ x 12⁸

Bedroom 11⁴ x 10⁸

Dining Room 12⁰ x 13⁰

Garage 22⁸ x 28⁰

Porch

Bedroom 11⁴ x 10⁸

Courtyard

plan⊕ HPT810110

STYLE: SANTA FE
SQUARE FOOTAGE: 2,032
BEDROOMS: 3
BATHROOMS: 2
WIDTH: 56'-4"
DEPTH: 70'-4"
FOUNDATION: SLAB

SEARCH ONLINE @ EPLANS.COM

A stepped stucco roof accen blends with Spanish tile for an eclecti spin on Southwestern style. A walle patio provides a lovely view from th formal dining room, just inside. Ope planning in the living areas expands th hearth-warmed great room, viewed fror an island kitchen overlook. At the rear, petite home office is adjacent to th bayed master suite, complete with a pr vate spa tub. Two secondary bedroom share a full bath toward the front of th home. The covered veranda offers yea round outdoor enjoyment.

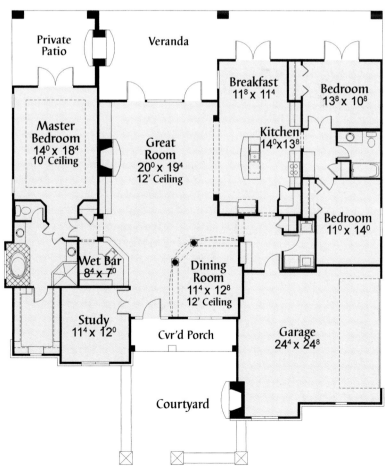

plan# HPT810111

STYLE: SW CONTEMPORARY
SQUARE FOOTAGE: 2,442
BEDROOMS: 3
BATHROOMS: 2
WIDTH: 64'-4"
DEPTH: 74'-6"
FOUNDATION: SLAB

SEARCH ONLINE @ EPLANS.COM

Stepped stucco blends with warm Spanish tile for a Southwestern home that enjoys a Mission-style influence. An outdoor fireplace begins the plan, luring guests to the main entry. A formal columned dining room is located on the right; conveniently close at hand, a wet bar enjoys a nine-foot ceiling. The great room is furnished with a fireplace framed by built-ins, which can be viewed from the kitchen's island. Two generous bedrooms inhabit the right side of the plan. The master suite is secluded to the left, enjoying a private hearth-warmed patio and a lavish bath.

plan⊕ HPT810112

STYLE: SW CONTEMPORARY
FIRST FLOOR: 1,768 SQ. FT.
SECOND FLOOR: 754 SQ. FT.
TOTAL: 2,522 SQ. FT.
BEDROOMS: 4
BATHROOMS: 4
WIDTH: 41'-0"
DEPTH: 75'-4"
FOUNDATION: SLAB

SEARCH ONLINE @ EPLANS.COM

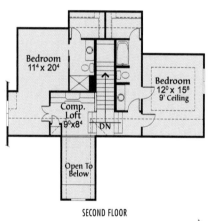

SECOND FLOOR

FIRST FLOOR

A classic Southwestern porch and Spanish tile roof blend fluidly with a contemporary dormer and prominent stucco facing for a one-of-a-kind home with tons of personal touches. Inside, the tiled entry continues past the box-bay living room to the angled-island kitchen. A ten-foot ceiling in the dinette and great room expands the space and a corner fireplace draws attention to a bright rear window wall. A box-vault in the master bedroom adds interest and French doors lead out to the veranda, complete with a fireplace. The private master bath features a garden tub and dual vanities.

plan# HPT810113

STYLE: SW CONTEMPORARY
SQUARE FOOTAGE: 2,014
BEDROOMS: 3
BATHROOMS: 2
WIDTH: 56'-4"
DEPTH: 70'-4"
FOUNDATION: SLAB

SEARCH ONLINE @ EPLANS.COM

A hipped roof faced with symmetrical gables lends an inviting first impression for this three-bedroom Sun Country home. Enter to find a formal dining room, defined by a column and outfitted with a buffet niche. Just ahead, an angled kitchen island views the great room's fireplace. A quaint cafe is perfect for casual meals and opens to the rear veranda. Past a modest home office, the bayed master suite offers a ten-foot box-vault ceiling and a private spa bath. Two additional bedrooms share a full bath near the entry.

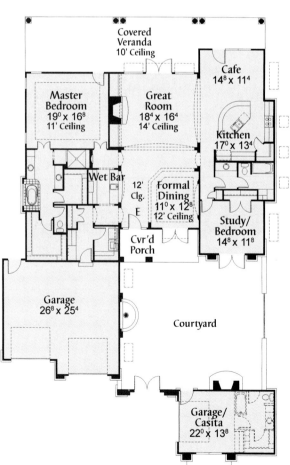

plan ⊕ HPT810114

STYLE: SW CONTEMPORARY
SQUARE FOOTAGE: 2,336
BONUS SPACE: 325 SQ. FT.
BEDROOMS: 2
BATHROOMS: 2
WIDTH: 63'-8"
DEPTH: 100'-4"
FOUNDATION: SLAB

SEARCH ONLINE @ EPLANS.COM

A stone-and-stucco facade makes this contemporary home a stand-out in any neighborhood. Almost every living area has outdoor access, creating an airy, sunlit atmosphere. At the front of the home, the dining room has an ornate trayed ceiling. The great room is perfect for any occasion, complete with a fireplace and built-ins. A wet bar is wonderful for entertaining. A rounded serving-bar island gives the kitchen a gourmet feel, and overlooks the casual "cafe." The nearby study/bedroom is adjacent to a full bath. In the exceptional master suite, an eleven-foot ceiling and luxurious spa bath will pamper and soothe. A convenient casita with an outdoor fireplace and optional full bath is ideal for guests.

TO ORDER BLUEPRINTS CALL TOLL FREE 1-800-521-679

plan# HPT810115

STYLE: SANTA FE
SQUARE FOOTAGE: 1,987
BEDROOMS: 2
BATHROOMS: 2
WIDTH: 49'-11"
DEPTH: 75'-4"
FOUNDATION: SLAB

SEARCH ONLINE @ EPLANS.COM

Southwestern style meets traditional family home in this updated casita.
Inside, twelve-foot ceilings crown most of
the living areas. The formal dining room
and hearth-warmed family room are
defined by tray ceilings. The island-
cooktop kitchen is open for increased
flow. The master suite features a box-vault
ceiling, access to the rear veranda and a
lavish bath. A bedroom at the front of the
home acts as a quiet study. The secluded
home office is brightened by a bayed wall.

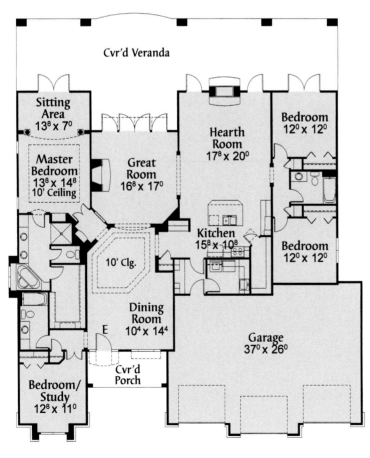

plan# HPT810116

STYLE: SW CONTEMPORARY
SQUARE FOOTAGE: 2,727
BEDROOMS: 4
BATHROOMS: 3
WIDTH: 68'-0"
DEPTH: 78'-0"
FOUNDATION: SLAB

SEARCH ONLINE @ EPLANS.COM

Stone accents and a front-facing three-car garage make a compelling presence for this contemporary home. Enter to a dining room on the right, lit by a tall picture window. A ten-foot hexagonal ceiling defines a sitting room or parlor area, perfect for entertaining. Continue through an arched opening to the great room, where four French doors lead to the rear veranda. The airy island kitchen views the hearth room's two-way fireplace. Nearby, twin bedrooms share a full bath. The master suite is embellished with a romantic sitting room and glorious spa bath. A bedroom/study at the front of the home makes an ideal guest room.

plan# HPT810117

STYLE: SW CONTEMPORARY
SQUARE FOOTAGE: 2,275
BEDROOMS: 3
BATHROOMS: 2
WIDTH: 58'-4"
DEPTH: 72'-8"
FOUNDATION: SLAB

SEARCH ONLINE @ EPLANS.COM

A unique arched entry makes a bold statement on this design. Inside, vast windows and multiple French doors fill the home with light. The great room and dining room are defined by elegant tray ceilings; a warming fireplace can be viewed by both areas. Don't miss the wet bar, perfect for entertaining. In the kitchen, an island contains the dual sink, expanding the workspace. Tucked to the rear for privacy, the master suite relishes a private covered patio (with a see-through fireplace!) and a marvelous bath with a corner whirlpool tub.

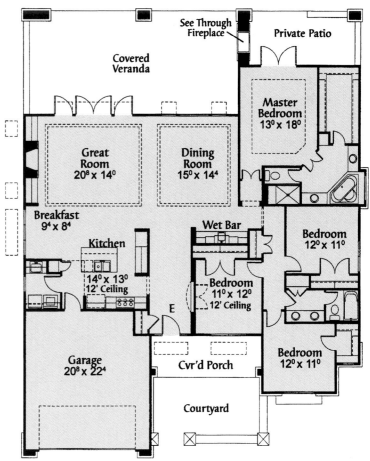

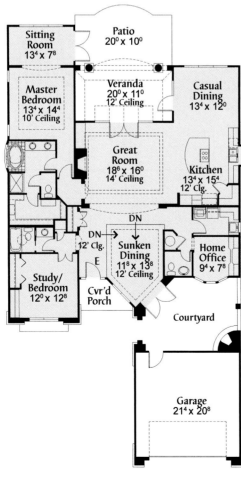

plan⊕ HPT810118

STYLE: SW CONTEMPORARY
SQUARE FOOTAGE: 2,097
BEDROOMS: 2
BATHROOMS: 2
WIDTH: 49'-4"
DEPTH: 79'-2"
FOUNDATION: SLAB

SEARCH ONLINE @ EPLANS.COM

Two bedrooms and two baths mak
this contemporary design the perfect starter c
empty-nest home. The sunken dining room, wit
a soaring twelve-foot ceiling, includes Frenc
doors that open to the courtyard. Nearby, th
kitchen includes a walk-in pantry and an islan
cooktop, which adjoins a casual dining are
with veranda access. The central great roon
which also opens to the veranda, includes a fir
place. Sleeping quarters—the master suite an
one secondary bedroom that can double as
study—reside to the left of the plan; the maste
suite includes a private sitting area with entry t
a rear patio. A home office, brightened by a ba
window, completes the plan.

plan# HPT810119

STYLE: SW CONTEMPORARY
SQUARE FOOTAGE: 2,430
BEDROOMS: 3
BATHROOMS: 2
WIDTH: 64'-4"
DEPTH: 74'-6"
FOUNDATION: SLAB

SEARCH ONLINE @ EPLANS.COM

A grand entry and Mission-style accents give this design great curb appeal. An outdoor fireplace in the front courtyard expands entertaining options. Inside, the trayed-ceiling dining room and stylish wet bar are ready to help you host your guests. Just ahead, the great room is filled with sunlight and enjoys the comfort of a warming fireplace, a natural gathering spot. The gourmet kitchen and breakfast nook are open and airy. Situated for peace and quiet, the master suite delights in French doors, set into a bay, leading to the rear veranda. A private spa bath accentuates the feeling of luxury. Generous secondary bedrooms at the right share a full bath.

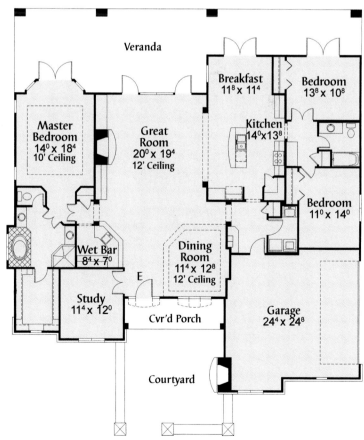

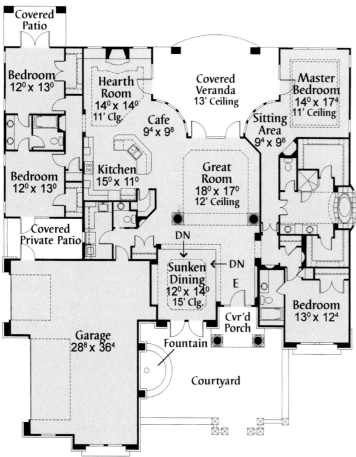

plan# HPT810120

STYLE: SW CONTEMPORARY
SQUARE FOOTAGE: 3,052
BEDROOMS: 4
BATHROOMS: 3½
WIDTH: 73'-0"
DEPTH: 87'-8"
FOUNDATION: SLAB

SEARCH ONLINE @ EPLANS.COM

A grand columned entry adorns th
facade of this contemporary Southwester
home. Tall windows, skylights and abundan
French doors allow floods of natural ligh
inside. The plan begins with a sunken dinin
room, topped by a fifteen-foot tray ceiling
Columns are echoed in the great room, wher
rear veranda access invites the outdoors in.
the kitchen, a boomerang-shaped island ove
looks the quaint "cafe" and cozy hearth roor
Bedrooms on the far left share a Jack-and-J
bath and access private patios. The maste
suite enjoys privacy, enhanced by a bowed si
ting room and sumptuous spa bath. A near
secondary bedroom has a private bath, and
perfect as a guest suite, home office, or nurser

plan# HPT810121

STYLE: SW CONTEMPORARY
SQUARE FOOTAGE: 3,226
BEDROOMS: 4
BATHROOMS: 3½
WIDTH: 72'-2"
DEPTH: 96'-8"
FOUNDATION: SLAB

SEARCH ONLINE @ EPLANS.COM

f you've been searching for a ontemporary design with today's most opular amenities, you're in luck! This lan has it all. A low-walled courtyard welomes family and guests to a grand entry. iside, the sunken dining room will npress, with a heightened ceiling and rench doors overlooking the fountain. ast the columned great room, the ngled-island kitchen is open to the "cafe" nd sunlit hearth room. The master suite a decadent retreat with a bowed sitting rea and exquisite spa bath. Ten-foot ceilgs in the walk-in closets are great for orage. All secondary bedrooms have rivate outdoor access.

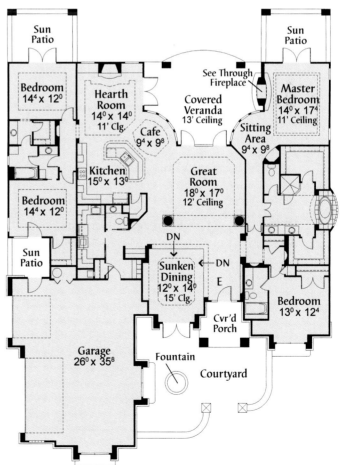

SECOND FLOOR

FIRST FLOOR

plan # HPT810122

STYLE: SW CONTEMPORARY
FIRST FLOOR: 1,316 SQ. FT.
SECOND FLOOR: 1,079 SQ. FT.
TOTAL: 2,395 SQ. FT.
BEDROOMS: 4
BATHROOMS: 2½
WIDTH: 49'-4"
DEPTH: 61'-0"
FOUNDATION: BASEMENT

SEARCH ONLINE @ EPLANS.COM

A multitude of windows adorns th
facade of this two-story, four-bedroom con
temporary design. Living quarters, located o
the first floor, include a study, great room
kitchen, hearth room and cafe. Fireplace
warm the great room and hearth room, and th
hearth room opens to the patio. A nearby fu
bath allows the study to serve as a bedroom
needed. Upstairs, the master suite includes
dual-vanity bath with a walk-in closet and se
arate tub and shower. Three additional be
rooms, each with plenty of closet space, sha
a full bath. A sunken bonus room can be deve
oped into computer or media room.

plan# HPT810123

STYLE: SW CONTEMPORARY
FIRST FLOOR: 2,260 SQ. FT.
SECOND FLOOR: 1,020 SQ. FT.
TOTAL: 3,280 SQ. FT.
BEDROOMS: 4
BATHROOMS: 3½
WIDTH: 69'-6"
DEPTH: 88'-2"
FOUNDATION: BASEMENT

SEARCH ONLINE @ EPLANS.COM

legant arched windows decorate
he facade of this two-story Southwestern
esign. Two fireplaces—one in the great
om and one in the hearth room—warm the
terior. Formal rooms—the dining room and
udy—sit to either side of the foyer. The
ficient kitchen boasts a walk-in pantry and
ljoins a cozy cafe area that opens to the
randa. The first-floor master suite includes
lavish private bath with dual vanities and a
alk-in closet, as well as a sitting area that
ens to a private patio. Upstairs, a home
fice joins three secondary bedrooms and
o full baths.

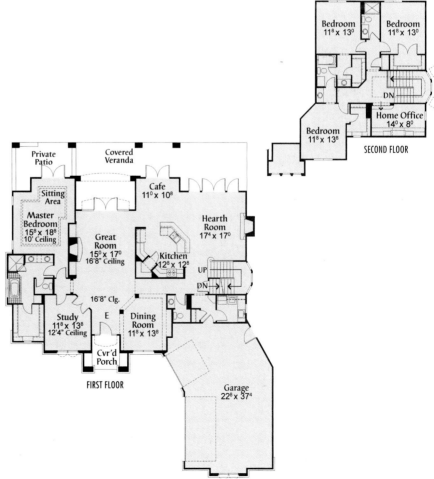

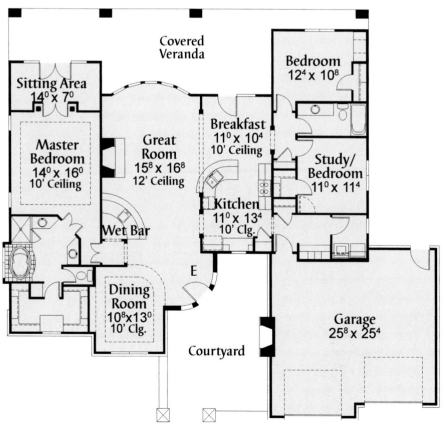

Sitting Area
14⁰ x 7⁰

Master Bedroom
14⁰ x 16⁰
10' Ceiling

Wet Bar

Covered Veranda

Great Room
15⁸ x 16⁸
12' Ceiling

Dining Room
10⁸ x 13⁰
10' Clg.

Courtyard

E

Breakfast
11⁰ x 10⁴
10' Ceiling

Kitchen
11⁰ x 13⁴
10' Clg.

Bedroom
12⁴ x 10⁸

Study/ Bedroom
11⁰ x 11⁴

Garage
25⁸ x 25⁴

plan# HPT810124

STYLE: SW CONTEMPORARY
SQUARE FOOTAGE: 1,950
BEDROOMS: 3
BATHROOMS: 2
WIDTH: 68'-0"
DEPTH: 62'-8"
FOUNDATION: SLAB

SEARCH ONLINE @ EPLANS.COM

A spacious entry courtyard introduces this contemporary Southwester[n] design. Inside, the formal dining room [is] placed to the left of the foyer; direct[ly] ahead, a wet bar sits at the entry of th[e] great room, which also boasts a fireplac[e] and a curved wall of windows. The nearb[y] kitchen shares a snack bar with the brea[k]fast area, which opens to a covered re[ar] veranda. Two bedrooms—one that c[an] double as a study—reside to the right [of] the plan; to the left, a charming mast[er] suite features a private bath, an expansi[ve] walk-in closet and a columned sitting are[a] that opens to the veranda.

eplans.com

THE GATEWAY
TO YOUR NEW HOME

Looking for more plans? Got questions?

Try our one-stop home plans resource—eplans.com.

We'll help you streamline the plan selection process, so your dreams can become reality faster than you ever imagined. From choosing your home plan and ideal location to finding an experienced contractor, eplans.com will guide you every step of the way.

Mix and match! Explore! At eplans.com you can combine all your top criteria to find your perfect match. Search for your ideal home plan by any or all of the following:

> Number of bedrooms or baths
> Total square feet
> House style
> Designer
> Cost

With over 10,000 plans, the options are endless. Colonial, ranch, country, and Victorian are just a few of the house styles offered. Keep in mind your essential lifestyle features—whether to include a porch, fireplace, bonus room or main floor laundry room. And the garage—how many cars must it accommodate, if any? By filling out the preference page on eplans.com, we'll help you narrow your search. And, don't forget to enjoy a virtual home tour before any decisions are set in stone.

At eplans.com we'll make the building process a snap to understand. At the click of a button you'll find a complete building guide. And our eplan task planner will create a construction calendar just for you. Here you'll find links to tips and other valuable information to help you every step of the way—from choosing a site to moving day.

For your added convenience, our home plans experts are available for live, one-on-one chats at eplans.com. Building a home may seem like a complicated project, but it doesn't have to be—particularly if you'll let us help you from start to finish.

COPYRIGHT DOS & DON'TS

Blueprints for residential construction (or working drawings, as they are often called in the industry) are copyrighted intellectual property, protected under the terms of United States Copyright Law and, therefore, cannot be copied legally for use in building. However, we've made it easy for you to get what you need to build your home, without violating copyright law. Following are some guidelines to help you obtain the right number of copies for your chosen blueprint design.

COPYRIGHT DO

■ Do purchase enough copies of the blueprints to satisfy building requirements. As a rule for a home or project plan, you will need a set for yourself, two or three for your builder and subcontractors, two for the local building department, and one to three for your mortgage lender. You may want to check with your local building department or your builder to see how many they need before you purchase. You may need to buy eight to 10 sets; note that some areas of the country require purchase of vellum (also called reproducibles) instead of blueprints. Vellums can be written on and changed more easily than blueprints. Also, remember, plans are only good for one-time construction.

■ Do consider reverse blueprints if you want to flop the plan. Lettering and numbering will appear backward, but the reversed set will help you and your builder better visualize the design.

■ Do take advantage of multiple-set discounts at the time you place your order. Usually, purchasing additional sets after you receive your initial order is not as cost-effective.

■ Do take advantage of vellums. Though they are a little more expensive, they can be changed, copied, and used for one-time construction of a home. You will receive a copyright release letter with your vellums that will allow you to have them copied.

■ Do talk with one of our professional service representatives before placing your order. They can give you great advice about what packages are available for your chosen design and what will work best for your particular situation.

COPYRIGHT DON'T

■ Don't think you should purchase only one set of blueprints for a building project. One is fine if you want to study the plan closely, but will not be enough for actual building.

■ Don't expect your builder or a copy center to make copies of standard blueprints. They cannot legally—most copy centers are aware of this.

■ Don't purchase standard blueprints if you know you'll want to make changes to the plan; vellums are a better value.

■ Don't use blueprints or vellums more than one time. Additional fees apply if you want to build more than one time from a set of drawings. ■

LET US SHOW YOU OUR HOME BLUEPRINT PACKAGE.

BUILDING A HOME? PLANNING A HOME?

OUR BLUEPRINT PACKAGE HAS NEARLY EVERYTHING YOU NEED TO GET THE JOB DONE RIGHT,

whether you're working on your own or with help from an architect, designer, builder or subcontractors. Each Blueprint Package is the result of many hours of work by licensed architects or professional designers.

QUALITY

Hundreds of hours of painstaking effort have gone into the development of your blueprint plan. Each home has been quality-checked by professionals to insure accuracy and buildability.

VALUE

Because we sell in volume, you can buy professional quality blueprints at a fraction of their development cost. With our plans, your dream home design costs substantially less than the fees charged by architects.

SERVICE

Once you've chosen your favorite home plan, you'll receive fast, efficient service whether you choose to mail or fax your order to us or call us toll free at 1-800-521-6797. After you have received your order, call for customer service toll free 1-888-690-1116.

SATISFACTION

Over 50 years of service to satisfied home plan buyers provide us unparalleled experience and knowledge in producing quality blueprints.

ORDER TOLL FREE 1-800-521-6797

After you've looked over our Blueprint Package and Important Extras, call toll free on our Blueprint Hotline: 1-800-521-6797, for current pricing and availability prior to mailing the order form on page 189. We're ready and eager to serve you. After you have received your order, call for customer service toll free 1-888-690-1116.

Each set of blueprints is an interrelated collection of detail sheets which includes components such as floor plans, interior and exterior elevations, dimensions, cross-sections, diagrams and notations. These sheets show exactly how your house is to be built.

SETS MAY INCLUDE:

FRONTAL SHEET
This artist's sketch of the exterior of the house gives you an idea of how the house will look when built and landscaped. Large floor plans show all levels of the house and provide an overview of your new home's livability, as well as a handy reference for deciding on furniture placement.

FOUNDATION PLANS
This sheet shows the foundation layout including support walls, excavated and unexcavated areas, if any, and foundation notes. If slab construction rather than basement, the plan shows footings and details for a monolithic slab. This page, or another in the set, may include a sample plot plan for locating your house on a building site.

DETAILED FLOOR PLANS
These plans show the layout of each floor of the house. Rooms and interior spaces are carefully dimensioned and keys are given for cross-section details provided later in the plans. The positions of electrical outlets and switches are shown.

HOUSE CROSS-SECTIONS
Large-scale views show sections or cut-aways of the foundation, interior walls, exterior walls, floors, stairways and roof details. Additional cross-sections may show important changes in floor, ceiling or roof heights or the relationship of one level to another. Extremely valuable for construction, these sections show exactly how the various parts of the house fit together.

INTERIOR ELEVATIONS
Many of our drawings show the design and placement of kitchen and bathroom cabinets, laundry areas, fireplaces, bookcases and other built-ins. Little "extras," such as mantelpiece and wainscoting drawings, plus molding sections, provide details that give your home that custom touch.

EXTERIOR ELEVATIONS
These drawings show the front, rear and sides of your house and give necessary notes on exterior materials and finishes. Particular attention is given to cornice detail, brick and stone accents or other finish items that make your home unique.

INTRODUCING IMPORTANT PLANNING AND CONSTRUCTION AIDS DEVELOPED BY OUR PROFESSIONALS TO HELP YOU SUCCEED IN YOUR HOME-BUILDING PROJECT

MATERIALS LIST

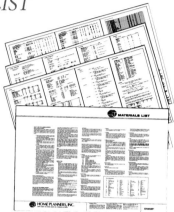

(Note: Because of the diversity of local building codes, our Materials List does not include mechanical materials.)

For many of the designs in our portfolio, we offer a customized materials take-off that is invaluable in planning and estimating the cost of your new home. This Materials List outlines the quantity, type and size of materials needed to build your house (with the exception of mechanical system items). Included are framing lumber, windows and doors, kitchen and bath cabinetry, rough and finish hardware, and much more. This handy list helps you or your builder cost out materials and serves as a reference sheet when you're compiling bids. Some Materials Lists may be ordered before blueprints are ordered, call for information.

SPECIFICATION OUTLINE

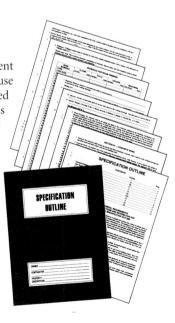

This valuable 16-page document is critical to building your house correctly. Designed to be filled in by you or your builder, this book lists 166 stages or items crucial to the building process. It provides a comprehensive review of the construction process and helps in choosing materials. When combined with the blueprints, a signed contract, and a schedule, it becomes a legal document and record for the building of your home.

QUOTE ONE®

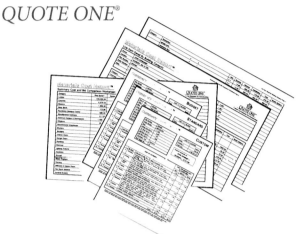

SUMMARY COST REPORT   **MATERIAL COST REPORT**

A product for estimating the cost of building select designs, the Quote One® system is available in two separate stages: The Summary Cost Report and the Material Cost Report.

The **Summary Cost Report** is the first stage in the package and shows the total cost per square foot for your chosen home in your zip-code area and then breaks that cost down into various categories showing the costs for building materials, labor and installation. The report includes three grades: Budget, Standard and Custom. These reports allow you to evaluate your building budget and compare the costs of building a variety of homes in your area.

Make even more informed decisions about your home-building project with the second phase of our package, our **Material Cost Report.** This tool is invaluable in planning and estimating the cost of your new home. The material and installation (labor and equipment) cost is shown for each of over 1,000 line items provided in the Materials List (Standard grade), which is included when you purchase this estimating tool. It allows you to determine building cost for your specific zip-code area and for your chosen home design. Space is allowed for additional estimates from contractors and subcontractors, such as for mechanical materials, which are not included in our packages. This invaluable tool includes a Materials List. A Material Cost Report cannot be ordered before blueprints are ordered. Call for details. In addition, ask about our Home Planners Estimating Package.

If you are interested in a plan that is not indicated as Quote One, please call and ask our sales reps. They will be happy to verify the status for you. To order these invaluable reports, use the order form.

CONSTRUCTION INFORMATION

IF YOU WANT TO KNOW MORE ABOUT TECHNIQUES—
and deal more confidently with subcontractors —
we offer these useful sheets. Each set is an excellent
tool that will add to your understanding of these
technical subjects. These helpful details provide
general construction information and
are not specific to any single plan.

PLUMBING

The Blueprint Package includes locations for all the plumbing fixtures, including sinks, lavatories, tubs, showers, toilets, laundry trays and water heaters. However, if you want to know more about the complete plumbing system, these Plumbing Details will prove very useful. Prepared to meet requirements of the National Plumbing Code, these fact-filled sheets give general information on pipe schedules, fittings, sump-pump details, water-softener hookups, septic system details and much more. Sheets also include a glossary of terms.

ELECTRICAL

The locations for every electrical switch, plug and outlet are shown in your Blueprint Package. However, these Electrical Details go further to take the mystery out of household electrical systems. Prepared to meet requirements of the National Electrical Code, these comprehensive drawings come packed with helpful information, including wire sizing, switch-installation schematics, cable-routing details, appliance wattage, doorbell hook-ups, typical service panel circuitry and much more. A glossary of terms is also included.

CONSTRUCTION

The Blueprint Package contains information an experienced builder needs to construct a particular house. However, it doesn't show all the ways that houses can be built, nor does it explain alternate construction methods. To help you understand how your house will be built—and offer additional techniques—this set of Construction Details depicts the materials and methods used to build foundations, fireplaces, walls, floors and roofs. Where appropriate, the drawings show acceptable alternatives.

MECHANICAL

These Mechanical Details contain fundamental principles and useful data that will help you make informed decisions and communicate with subcontractors about heating and cooling systems. Drawings contain instructions and samples that allow you to make simple load calculations, and preliminary sizing and costing analysis. Covered are the most commonly used systems from heat pumps to solar fuel systems. The package is filled with illustrations and diagrams to help you visualize components and how they relate to one another.

THE HANDS-ON HOME FURNITURE PLANNER

Effectively plan the space in your home using The **Hands-On Home Furniture Planner**. It's fun and easy—no more moving heavy pieces of furniture to see how the room will go together. And you can try different layouts, moving furniture at a whim.

The kit includes reusable peel and stick furniture templates that fit onto a 12" x 18" laminated layout board—space enough to layout every room in your home.

Also included in the package are a number of helpful planning tools. You'll receive:

✓ Helpful hints and solutions for difficult situations.
✓ Furniture planning basics to get you started.
✓ Furniture planning secrets that let you in on some of the tricks of professional designers.

The **Hands-On Home Furniture Planner** is the one tool that no new homeowner or home remodeler should be without. It's also a perfect housewarming gift!

To Order, Call Toll Free
1-800-521-6797

After you've looked over our Blueprint Package and Important Extras on these pages, call for current pricing and availability prior to mailing the order form. We're ready and eager to serve you. After you have received your order, call for customer service toll free 1-888-690-1116.

THE FINISHING TOUCHES...

THE DECK BLUEPRINT PACKAGE

Many of the homes in this book can be enhanced with a professionally designed Home Planners Deck Plan. Those homes marked with a **D** have a complementary Deck Plan, sold separately, which includes a Deck Plan Frontal Sheet, Deck Framing and Floor Plans, Deck Elevations and a Deck Materials List. A Standard Deck Details Package, also available, provides all the how-to information necessary for building *any* deck. Our Complete Deck Building Package contains one set of Custom Deck Plans of your choice, plus one set of Standard Deck Building Details, all for one low price. Our plans and details are carefully prepared in an easy-to-understand format that will guide you through every stage of your deck-building project. This page shows a sample Deck layout to match your favorite house. See Blueprint Price Schedule for ordering information.

THE LANDSCAPE BLUEPRINT PACKAGE

For the homes marked with an **L** in this book, Home Planners has created a front-yard Landscape Plan that is complementary in design to the house plan. These comprehensive blueprint packages include a Frontal Sheet, Plan View, Regionalized Plant & Materials List, a sheet on Planting and Maintaining Your Landscape, Zone Maps and Plant Size and Description Guide. These plans will help you achieve professional results, adding value and enjoyment to your property for years to come. Each set of blueprints is a full 18" x 24" in size with clear, complete instructions and easy-to-read type. A sample Landscape Plan is shown below. See Blueprint Price Schedule for ordering information.

CONTEMPORARY LEISURE DECK
Deck ODA021

CAPE COD COTTAGE
Landscape OLA003

REGIONAL ORDER MAP

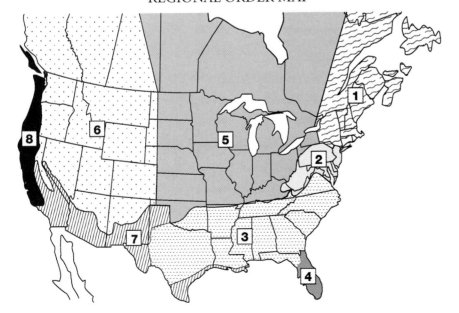

Most Landscape Plans are available with Plant & Materials List adapted by horticultural experts to 8 different regions of the country. Please specify the Geographic Region when ordering your plan. See Blueprint Price Schedule for ordering information and regional availability.

Region	1	Northeast
Region	2	Mid-Atlantic
Region	3	Deep South
Region	4	Florida & Gulf Coast
Region	5	Midwest
Region	6	Rocky Mountains
Region	7	Southern California & Desert Southwest
Region	8	Northern California & Pacific Northwest

184 **SOUTHWEST INSPIRATION**   TO ORDER BLUEPRINTS PHONE TOLL FREE 1-800-521-67

BLUEPRINT PRICE SCHEDULE

Prices guaranteed through December 31, 2003

TIERS	1-SET STUDY PACKAGE	4-SET BUILDING PACKAGE	8-SET BUILDING PACKAGE	1-SET REPRODUCIBLE*
P1	$20	$50	$90	$140
P2	$40	$70	$110	$160
P3	$70	$100	$140	$190
P4	$100	$130	$170	$220
P5	$140	$170	$210	$270
P6	$180	$210	$250	$310
A1	$440	$480	$520	$660
A2	$480	$520	$560	$720
A3	$530	$575	$615	$800
A4	$575	$620	$660	$870
C1	$620	$665	$710	$935
C2	$670	$715	$760	$1000
C3	$715	$760	$805	$1075
C4	$765	$810	$855	$1150
L1	$870	$925	$975	$1300
L2	$945	$1000	$1050	$1420
L3	$1050	$1105	$1155	$1575
L4	$1155	$1210	$1260	$1735
SQ1				.35/sq. ft.

* Requires a fax number

[OP]TIONS FOR PLANS IN TIERS A1–L4

[Addi]tional Identical Blueprints
[in sa]me order for "A1–L4" price plans ....$50 per set
[Reve]rse Blueprints (mirror image)
[in] 4- or 8-set order for "A1–L4" plans ....$50 fee per order
[Spec]ification Outlines ....$10 each
[Mat]erials Lists for "A1–C3" plans ....$60 each
[Mat]erials Lists for "C4–SQ1" plans ....$70 each

OPTIONS FOR PLANS IN TIERS P1–P6

Additional Identical Blueprints
in same order for "P1–P6" price plans ....$10 per set
Reverse Blueprints (mirror image) for "P1–P6" price plans ....$10 fee per order
1 Set of Deck Construction Details...$14.95 each
Deck Construction Package ....**add $10 to Building Package price**
(includes 1 set of "P1–P6" plans, plus
1 set Standard Deck Construction Details)

[IMP]ORTANT NOTES

[A] one-set building package includes one set of reproducible vellum
[con]struction drawings plus one set of study blueprints.
[The] 1-set study package is marked "not for construction."
[Pric]es for 4- or 8-set Building Packages honored only at time of original order.
[Ston]e foundations carry a $225 surcharge.
[Rig]ht-reading reverse blueprints, if available, will incur a $165 surcharge.
[Add]itional identical blueprints may be purchased within 60 days of original order.

[T]O USE THE INDEX,

[Ref]er to the design number listed in numerical order (a helpful page ref-
[ere]nce is also given). Note the price tier and refer to the Blueprint Price
[Sch]edule above for the cost of one, four or eight sets of blueprints or the
[cos]t of a reproducible drawing. Additional prices are shown for identical
[and] reverse blueprint sets, as well as a very useful Materials List for some
[of t]he plans. Also note in the Plan Index those plans that have Deck Plans
[or L]andscape Plans. Refer to the schedules above for prices of these plans.
[Th]e letter "Y" identifies plans that are part of our Quote One® estimating
[ser]vice and those that offer Materials Lists.

[T]O ORDER,

[Cal]l toll free 1-800-521-6797 for current pricing and availability prior to
[mai]ling the order form. FAX: 1-800-224-6699 or 520-544-3086.

PLAN INDEX

DESIGN	PRICE	PAGE	MATERIALS LIST	QUOTE ONE®	DECK	DECK PRICE	LANDSCAPE	LANDSCAPE PRICE	REGIONS
HPT810001	C3	25	Y	Y			OLA037	P4	347
HPT810002	C4	29	Y	Y	ODA010	P3	OLA021	P3	123568
HPT810003	C3	34	Y	Y			OLA038	P3	7
HPT810004	C1	39	Y	Y			OLA014	P4	12345678
HPT810005	C1	44	Y	Y			OLA040	P4	123467
HPT810006	L1	50	Y	Y			OLA037	P4	347
HPT810007	C4	51	Y	Y					

BEFORE FILLING OUT

THE ORDER FORM,

PLEASE CALL US ON

OUR TOLL-FREE

BLUEPRINT HOTLINE

1-800-521-6797.

YOU MAY WANT TO

LEARN MORE ABOUT

OUR SERVICES AND

PRODUCTS. HERE'S

SOME INFORMATION

YOU WILL FIND HELPFUL.

OUR EXCHANGE POLICY

With the exception of reproducible plan orders, we will exchange your entire first order for an equal or greater number of blueprints within our plan collection within 90 days of the original order. The entire content of your original order must be returned before an exchange will be processed. Please call our customer service department for your return authorization number and shipping instructions. If the returned blueprints look used, redlined or copied, we will not honor your exchange. Fees for exchanging your blueprints are as follows: 20% of the amount of the original order...plus the difference in cost if exchanging for a design in a higher price bracket or less the difference in cost if exchanging for a design in a lower price bracket. (**Reproducible blueprints are not exchangeable or refundable.**) Please call for current postage and handling prices. Shipping and handling charges are not refundable.

ABOUT REPRODUCIBLES

When purchasing a reproducible you may be required to furnish a fax number. The designer will fax documents that you must sign and return to them before shipping will take place.

ABOUT REVERSE BLUEPRINTS

Although lettering and dimensions will appear backward, reverses will be a useful aid if you decide to flop the plan. See Price Schedule and Plans Index for pricing.

REVISING, MODIFYING
AND CUSTOMIZING PLANS

Like many homeowners who buy these plans, you and your builder, architect or engineer may want to make changes to them. We recommend purchase of a reproducible plan for any changes made by your builder, licensed architect or engineer. As set forth below, we cannot assume any responsibility for blueprints which have been changed, whether by you, your builder or by professionals selected by you or referred to you by us, because such individuals are outside our supervision and control.

ARCHITECTURAL
AND ENGINEERING SEALS

Some cities and states are now requiring that a licensed architect or engineer review and "seal" a blueprint, or officially approve it, prior to construction due to concerns over energy costs, safety and other factors. Prior to application for a building permit or the start of actual construction, we strongly advise that you consult your local building official who can tell you if such a review is required.

ABOUT THE DESIGNS

The architects and designers whose work appears in this publication are among America's leading residential designers. Each plan was designed to meet the requirements of a nationally recognized model building code in effect at the time and place the plan was drawn. Because national building codes change from time to time, plans may not comply with any such code at the time they are sold to a customer. In addition, building officials may not accept these plans as final construction documents of record as the plans may need to be modified and additional drawings and details added to suit local conditions and requirements. We strongly advise that purchasers consult a licensed architect or engineer, and their local building official, before starting any construction related to these plans.

LOCAL BUILDING CODES
AND ZONING REQUIREMENTS

At the time of creation, our plans are drawn to specifications published by the Building Officials and Code Administrators (BOCA) International, Inc.; the Southern Building Code Congress (SBCCI) International, Inc.; the International Conference of Building Officials (ICBO); or the Council of American Building Officials (CABO). Our plans are designed to meet or exceed national building standards. Because of the great differences in geography and climate throughout the United States and Canada, each state, county and municipality has its own building codes, zone requirements, ordinances and building regulations. Your plan may need to be modified to comply with local requirements regarding snow loads, energy codes, soil and seismic conditions and a wide range of other matters. In addition, you may need to obtain permits or inspections from local governments before and in the course of construction. Prior to using blueprints ordered from us, we strongly advise that you consult a licensed architect or engineer—and speak with your local building official—before applying for any permit or beginning construction. We authorize the use of our blueprints on the express condition that you strictly comply with all local building codes, zoning requirements and other applicable laws, regulations, ordinances and requirements. Notice: Plans for homes to be built in Nevada must be re-drawn by a Nevada-registered professional. Consult your building official for more information on this subject.

TOLL FREE
1-800-521-6797

REGULAR OFFICE HOURS:
8:00 a.m.-9:00 p.m. EST, Monday-Friday

If we receive your order by 3:00 p.m. EST, Monday-Friday, we'll process it and ship within **two business days**. When ordering by phone, please have your credit card or check information ready. We'll also ask you for the Order Form Key Number at the bottom of the order form.

By FAX: Copy the Order Form on the next page and send it on our FAX line: 1-800-224-6699 or 520-544-3086.

Canadian Customers
Order Toll Free 1-877-223-6389

DISCLAIMER

The designers we work with have put substantial care and effort into the creation of their blueprints. However, because they cannot provide on-site consultation, supervision and control over actual construction, and because of the great variance in local building requirements, building practices and soil, seismic, weather and other conditions, WE CANNOT MAKE ANY WARRANTY, EXPRESS OR IMPLIED, WITH RESPECT TO THE CONTENT OR USE OF THE BLUEPRINTS, INCLUDING BUT NOT LIMITED TO ANY WARRANTY OF MERCHANTABILITY OR OF FITNESS FOR A PARTICULAR PURPOSE. **ITEMS, PRICES, TERMS AND CONDITIONS ARE SUBJECT TO CHANGE WITHOUT NOTICE. REPRODUCIBLE PLAN ORDERS MAY REQUIRE A CUSTOMER'S SIGNED RELEASE BEFORE SHIPPING.**

TERMS AND CONDITIONS

These designs are protected under the terms of United States Copyright Law and may not be copied or reproduced in any way, by any means, unless you have purchased Reproducibles which clearly indicate your right to copy or reproduce. We authorize the use of your chosen design as an aid in the construction of one single family home only. You may not use this design to build a second or multiple dwellings without purchasing another blueprint or blueprints or paying additional design fees.

HOW MANY BLUEPRINTS DO YOU NEED?

Although a standard building package may satisfy many states, cities and counties, some plans may require certain changes. For your convenience, we have developed a Reproducible plan which allows a local professional to modify and make up to 10 copies of your revised plan. As our plans are all copyright protected, with your purchase of the Reproducible, we will supply you with a Copyright release letter. The number of copies you may need: 1 for owner; 3 for builder; 2 for local building department and 1-3 sets for your mortgage lender.

ORDER TOLL FREE!

**For information about
any of our services
or to order call
1-800-521-6797**

**Browse our website:
www.eplans.com**

**BLUEPRINTS ARE
NOT REFUNDABLE
EXCHANGES ONLY**

**For Customer Service,
call toll free
1-888-690-1116.**

HOME PLANNERS, LLC wholly owned by Hanley-Wood, LLC
3275 WEST INA ROAD, SUITE 220 • TUCSON, ARIZONA • 85741

THE BASIC BLUEPRINT PACKAGE
Rush me the following (please refer to the Plans Index and Price Schedule in this section):
____ Set(s) of reproducibles*, plan number(s) _____ $_____
    indicate foundation type _____ surcharge (if applicable): $_____
____ Set(s) of blueprints, plan number(s) _____ indicate foundation type _____
    indicate foundation type _____ surcharge (if applicable): $_____
____ Additional identical blueprints (standard or reverse) in same order @ $50 per set $_____
____ Reverse blueprints @ $50 fee per order. Right-reading reverse @ $165 surcharge $_____

IMPORTANT EXTRAS
Rush me the following:
____ Materials List: $60 (Must be purchased with Blueprint set.) Add $10 for Schedule C4–SQ1 plans $_____
____ **Quote One®** Summary Cost Report @ $29.95 for one, $14.95 for each additional,
    for plans _____ $_____
    Building location: City _____ Zip Code _____
____ **Quote One®** Material Cost Report @ $120 Schedules P1–C3; $130 Schedules C4–SQ1,
    for plan _____ (Must be purchased with Blueprints set.) $_____
    Building location: City _____ Zip Code _____
____ Specification Outlines @ $10 each $_____
____ Detail Sets @ $14.95 each; any two $22.95; any three $29.95; all four for $39.95 (save $19.85) $_____
    ❑ Plumbing ❑ Electrical ❑ Construction ❑ Mechanical
____ Home Furniture Planner @ $15.95 each $_____

DECK BLUEPRINTS
(Please refer to the Plans Index and Price Schedule in this section)
____ Set(s) of Deck Plan _____. $_____
____ Additional identical blueprints in same order @ $10 per set. $_____
____ Reverse blueprints @ $10 fee per order. $_____
____ Set of Standard Deck Details @ $14.95 per set. $_____
____ Set of Complete Deck Construction Package (Best Buy!) Add $10 to Building Package.
    Includes Custom Deck Plan _____ Plus Standard Deck Details

LANDSCAPE BLUEPRINTS
(Please refer to the Plans Index and Price Schedule in this section.)
____ Set(s) of Landscape Plan _____ $_____
____ Additional identical blueprints in same order @ $10 per set $_____
____ Reverse blueprints @ $10 fee per order $_____
Please indicate appropriate region of the country for Plant & Material List. Region _____

POSTAGE AND HANDLING *SIGNATURE IS REQUIRED FOR ALL DELIVERIES.*	1–3 sets	4+ sets
DELIVERY No CODs (Requires street address—No P.O. Boxes) •Regular Service (Allow 7–10 business days delivery) •Priority (Allow 4–5 business days delivery) •Express (Allow 3 business days delivery)	 ❑ $20.00 ❑ $25.00 ❑ $35.00	 ❑ $25.00 ❑ $35.00 ❑ $45.00
OVERSEAS DELIVERY	fax, phone or mail for quote	

Note: All delivery times are from date Blueprint Package is shipped.

POSTAGE (From box above) $_____
SUBTOTAL $_____
SALES TAX (AZ & MI residents, please add appropriate state and local sales tax.) $_____
TOTAL (Subtotal and tax) $_____

YOUR ADDRESS (please print legibly)
Name _____
Street _____
City _____ State _____ Zip _____
Daytime telephone number (required) (_____) _____
* Fax number (required for reproducible orders) _____
TeleCheck® Checks By Phone℠ available
FOR CREDIT CARD ORDERS ONLY
Credit card number _____ Exp. Date: (M/Y) _____
Check one ❑ Visa ❑ MasterCard ❑ American Express

Order Form Key

HPT81

Signature (required)_____
Please check appropriate box: ❑ Licensed Builder-Contractor ❑ Homeowner

ORDER TOLL FREE!
1-800-521-6797

BY FAX: Copy the order form above and send it on our FAXLINE: 1-800-224-6699 OR 520-544-3086

1 BIGGEST & BEST

1001 of our best-selling plans in one volume. 1,074 to 7,275 square feet. 704 pgs $12.95 1K1

2 ONE-STORY

450 designs for all lifestyles. 800 to 4,900 square feet. 384 pgs $9.95 OS

3 MORE ONE-STORY

475 superb one-level plans from 800 to 5,000 square feet. 448 pgs $9.95 MO2

4 TWO-STORY

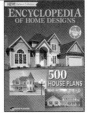

443 designs for one-and-a-half and two stories. 1,500 to 6,000 square feet. 448 pgs $9.95 TS

5 VACATION

430 designs for recreation, retirement and leisure. 448 pgs $9.95 VS3

6 HILLSIDE

208 designs for split-levels, bi-levels, multi-levels and walk-outs. 224 pgs $9.95 HH

7 FARMHOUSE

300 Fresh Designs from Classic to Modern. 320 pgs. $10.95 FCP

8 COUNTRY HOUSES

208 unique home plans that combine traditional style and modern livability. 224 pgs $9.95 CN

9 BUDGET-SMART

200 efficient plans from 7 top designers, that you can really afford to build! 224 pgs $8.95 BS

10 BARRIER-FREE

Over 1,700 products and 51 plans for accessible living. 128 pgs $15.95 UH

11 ENCYCLOPEDIA

500 exceptional plans for all styles and budgets—the best book of its kind! 528 pgs $9.95 ENC

12 ENCYCLOPEDIA II

500 completely new plans. Spacious and stylish designs for every budget and taste. 352 pgs $9.95 E2

13 AFFORDABLE

300 Modest plans for savvy homebuyers.256 pgs. $9.95 AH2

14 VICTORIAN

210 striking Victorian and Farmhouse designs from today's top designers. 224 pgs $15.95 VDH2

15 ESTATE

Dream big! Eighteen designers showcase their biggest and best plans. 224 pgs $16.95 EDH3

16 LUXURY

170 lavish designs, over 50% brand-new plans added to a most elegant collection. 192 pgs $12.95 LD3

17 EUROPEAN STYLES

200 homes with a unique flair of the Old World. 224 pgs $15.95 EURO

18 COUNTRY CLASSICS

Donald Gardner's 101 best Country and Traditional home plans. 192 pgs $17.95 DAG

19 COUNTRY

85 Charming Designs from American Home Gallery. 160 pgs. $17.95 CTY

20 TRADITIONAL

85 timeless designs from the Design Traditions Library. 160 pgs. $17.95 TRA

21 COTTAGES

245 Delightful retreats from 825 to 3,500 square feet. 256 pgs. $10.95 COOL

22 CABINS TO VILLAS

Enchanting Homes for Mountain Sea or Sun, from the Sater collection. 144 pgs $19.95 CCV

23 CONTEMPORARY

The most complete and imagi-native collection of contempo-rary designs available anywhere. 256 pgs. $10.95 CM2

24 FRENCH COUNTRY

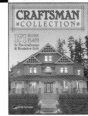

Live every day in the French countryside using these plans, landscapes and interiors. 192 pgs. $14.95 PN

25 SOUTHERN

207 homes rich in Southern styling and comfort. 240 pgs $8.95 SH

26 SOUTHWESTERN

138 designs that capture the spirit of the Southwest. 144 pgs $10.95 SW

27 SHINGLE-STYLE

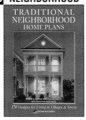

155 Home plans from Classic Colonials to Breezy Bungalows. 192 pgs. $12.95 SNG

28 NEIGHBORHOOD

170 designs with the feel of main street America. 192 pgs $12.95 TND

29 CRAFTSMAN

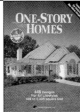

170 Home plans in the Craftsman and Bungalow style. 192 pgs $12.95 CC

30 GRAND VISTAS

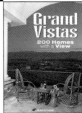

200 Homes with a View. 224 pgs. $10.95 GV

31 DUPLEX & TOWNHOMES

115 Duplex, Multiplex & Townhome Designs. 128 pgs. $17.95 MFH

32 WATERFRONT

200 designs perfect for your waterside wonderland. 208 pgs $10.95 WF

33 NATURAL LIGHT

223 Sunny home plans for all regions. 240 pgs. $8.95 NA

34 NOSTALGIA

100 Time-Honored designs updated with today's features. 224 pgs. $14.95 NOS

35 STREET OF DREAMS

Over 300 photos showcase 54 prestigious homes. 256 pgs $19.95 SOD

36 NARROW-LOT

250 Designs for houses 17' to 50' wide. 256 pgs. $9.95 NL2

37 SMALL HOUSES
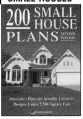
Innovative plans for sensible lifestyles. 224 pgs. $8.95 SM2

38 GARDENS & MORE

225 gardens, landscapes, decks and more to enhance every home. 320 pgs. $19.95 GLP

39 EASY-CARE

41 special landscapes designed for beauty and low maintenance. 160 pgs $14.95 ECL

40 BACKYARDS

40 designs focused solely on creating your own specially themed backyard oasis. 160 pgs $14.95 BYL

41 BEDS & BORDERS

40 Professional designs for do-it-yourselfers 160 pgs. $14.95 BB

42 BUYER'S GUIDE

A comprehensive look at 2700 products for all aspects of landscaping & gardening. 128 pgs $19.95 LPBG

LANDSCAPE DESIGNS

43 OUTDOOR

74 easy-to-build designs, lets you create and build your own backyard oasis. 128 pgs $9.95 YG2

44 GARAGES

145 exciting projects from 64 to 1,900 square feet. 160 pgs. $9.95 GG2

45 DECKS

A brand new collection of 120 beautiful and practical decks. 144 pgs. $9.95 DP2

46 HOME BUILDING

Everything you need to know to work with contractors and subcontractors. 212 pgs $14.95 HBP

47 RURAL BUILDING

Everything you need to know to build your home in the country. 232 pgs. $14.95 BYC

48 VACATION HOMES

Your complete guide to building your vacation home. 224 pgs. $14.95 BYV

PROJECT GUIDES

Book Order Form

To order your books, just check the box of the book numbered below and complete the coupon. We will process your order and ship it from our office within two business days. Send coupon and check (in U.S. funds).

YES! Please send me the books I've indicated:

❏ 1:1K1.........$12.95	❏ 17:EURO ...$15.95	❏ 33:NA $8.95
❏ 2:OS $9.95	❏ 18:DAG.....$17.95	❏ 34:NOS.....$14.95
❏ 3:MO2.....$9.95	❏ 19:CTY.....$17.95	❏ 35:SOD.....$19.95
❏ 4:TS............$9.95	❏ 20:TRA......$17.95	❏ 36:NL2.......$9.95
❏ 5:VS3...........$9.95	❏ 21:COOL....$10.95	❏ 37:SM2.......$8.95
❏ 6:HH...........$9.95	❏ 22:CCV $19.95	❏ 38:GLP.....$19.95
❏ 7:FCP.....$10.95	❏ 23:CM2.....$10.95	❏ 39:ECL.....$14.95
❏ 8:CN............$9.95	❏ 24:PN......$14.95	❏ 40:BYL.....$14.95
❏ 9:BS............$8.95	❏ 25:SH $8.95	❏ 41:BB $14.95
❏ 10:UH.....$15.95	❏ 26:SW $10.95	❏ 42:LPBG...$19.95
❏ 11:ENC.......$9.95	❏ 27:SNG.....$12.95	❏ 43:YG2.......$9.95
❏ 12:E2.......$9.95	❏ 28:TND.....$12.95	❏ 44:GG2.......$9.95
❏ 13:AH2.......$9.95	❏ 29:CC $12.95	❏ 45:DP2.......$9.95
❏ 14:VDH2....$15.95	❏ 30:GV $10.95	❏ 46:HBP.....$14.95
❏ 15:EDH3....$16.95	❏ 31:MFH $17.95	❏ 47:BYC.....$14.95
❏ 16:LD3.....$12.95	❏ 32:WF $10.95	❏ 48:BYV.....$14.95

Books Subtotal $_____
ADD Postage and Handling (allow 4–6 weeks for delivery) $ 4.00
Sales Tax: (AZ & MI residents, add state and local sales tax.) $_____
YOUR TOTAL (Subtotal, Postage/Handling, Tax) $_____

YOUR ADDRESS (PLEASE PRINT)
Name_____
Street _____
City _____ State_____ Zip _____
Phone (_____) _____—_____

YOUR PAYMENT
TeleCheck® Checks By Phone℠ available
Check one: ❏ Check ❏ Visa ❏ MasterCard ❏ American Express
Required credit card information:
Credit Card Number_____
Expiration Date (Month/Year)   /
Signature Required _____

Home Planners, LLC
3275 W. Ina Road, Suite 220, Dept. BK, Tucson, AZ 85741

HPT81

Canadian Customers Order Toll Free 1-877-223-6389